ADVANCE REVIEWS

Eloquent and elegant, this wonderful and wise book digs deep into what it means to parent from the heart. It will open you up to an entirely new way of raising children. Heartwarming and insightful, Cathy Adams invites you to explore your most authentic self through your parenting.

DR. SHEFALI TSABARY
Clinical Psychologist and Best-Selling Author of *The Conscious Parent*

Straight from the heart, Cathy Adams invites parents to actually live what they are guiding their children to become-emotionally whole individuals who embody self-awareness. With a deep sense of what is real and true, this book offers an intimate glimpse into a mother's desire to navigate life from a place where her interior is authentically expressed in her daily life. Modeling this type of inside-out living, true integrity, is perhaps the greatest gift parents can offer their children. A simple and profound book that will move you deeply!

ANNIE BURNSIDE
Award-winning Author of *Soul to Soul Parenting* and *From Role to Soul*

This book is a lifelong companion! A source sharing homemade insights AND scholarly wisdom, each page inspires and enlightens. Cathy's personal and parenting reflections stream from the heart and remind us that we are not alone in our challenging moments. Her messages comfort the soul while encouraging parents to be aware and know joy as presence. Open the book to any page. What you read will be a gift to yourself and your children.

ALEXANDRA FOLZ, MSN
Author of *Indigo's Bracelet, Indigo's Crystals,*
Indigo's Wings – The Heirloom Trilogy

I have been a fan of Cathy Adams Cassani for years. I appreciate her insight, humor and simplicity—she helps me stay present, assess what's really important, and she offers tools on how to act and react, especially during those times when I'm questioning myself. Listening and learning from Cathy has helped give me the confidence and tools to be more comfortable in my own skin. I accept that I'm not perfect, but I also know that who I am as a woman, mother, friend, daughter, wife, is the best I can be—*right here, right now*. I love this quote from her: "All we can do is make the best choice we know for this moment right now. It's unwise to plan too far ahead, and it certainly isn't helpful to hold onto past mistakes. We have to embrace our own present-moment clarity, making the best game-time decisions we know to make with the information we have at present." Thank you Cathy for writing this book and for allowing me to have all of your wisdom at my fingertips. You are a positive force for change and awareness in every aspect of our lives. This book reminded me that "living life is a practice", and I know I'm getting better at it.

JILL DAILEY MCINTOSH
Founder of The Dailey Method

The challenge of balancing work and family in today's environment requires us to slow down and think about how we parent consciously while meeting our obligations at the office. This book provides great insight, reminders, and tools to help parents become good examples for their children.

AMY RODGERS
VP Global Human Resources, Working Mother and Blogger,
Chicago Working Women

There are few books that move me to heartfelt tears and remind me of my own greatness along the way, but Cathy's book did just that. She has opened her heart and shared her life so that we can be reminded of love, acceptance, and courage that resides in each and every one of us. Story after story I experienced a lump in my throat, tears in my eyes, and love in my heart. Her words have the power to uplift a tired mom, inspire a hopeful dad, appreciate a dedicated grandparent, and most importantly, remind our children of their greatness. Cathy is here on purpose. She is sharing her wisdom and love to remind us all of the power that lives in each and every one of us. As I finished the last paragraph in the book, I felt understood, empowered, valued, inspired, and enlightened. She is a gift to our planet.

HEATHER CRISWELL
Founder of WiseInside

Every mother should read this book! Cathy Adams gives us the wisdom and perspective that mamas need. While it includes great specific parenting tips and stories, the power of this book is how Cathy points us again and again to the bigger picture. Why we should live with truth, clarity, and awareness. Why our own self-care is so important. Why we have to become the change we want to see. Why we must practice kindness, respect, and love for ourselves if we want our children to learn kindness, respect, and love. This book will help mothers, new and experienced, reach a new level of self-understanding. This benefits our families, our communities, and the world. Cathy balances refreshing honesty with an undeterred positive outlook that makes this book a must beside every mama's bedside.

HUNTER CLARKE-FIELDS
Yoga & Mindfulness Coach for mamas at HunterYoga.com

I read and enjoyed both of Cathy's previous books, but *Living What You Want Your Kids to Learn* is simply a masterpiece. It is filled with stories and ideas that I could relate to as a mother, therapist and PCI Certified Parent Coach®. I "discovered" Cathy several years ago, back in the early days of the Zen Parenting

Radio podcast that she does with her husband, Todd. It is both surprising and comforting that someone I have admired for so long struggled with the same frustrations I did in the early days of motherhood. I know how much I would have cherished her book if it had existed when my oldest child was born. I found myself smiling and nodding in enthusiastic agreement when I read about her experience of loss through miscarriage, her daughter not wanting to dance in the recital, and her response to chaos being her wanting to do things herself. Cathy's warm, engaging writing style feels to the reader like sitting down with a dear friend for coffee. Her heart-centered way of teaching through storytelling made me feel many times throughout the book as if she was speaking directly to me, and I am certain that parents from all walks of life will feel exactly the same when they read this wonderful book. Cathy is a parent and a person who is wise well beyond her years. This treasure is a must-read for all parents, no matter what ages their children are. I will be adding this to all the baby shower gifts I give from now on!

ERIN TAYLOR, MA
Mother, PCI Certified Parent Coach® and Therapist

A thought-provoking and caring book full of practical tips for today's parents. With her genuine voice and use of heartfelt stories, Cathy beautifully articulates the challenges and benefits of becoming a self-aware person and parent.

MARY ELLEN YOUNG
Author of *ELEMENTS for girls*

Cathy Cassani Adams has done it again. In her new book, *Living What You Want Your Kids to Learn*, Cathy gently yet powerfully invites us to grow in self-awareness. She intimately and generously shares her parenting and life experiences with her readers. Cathy addresses head-on the power of acknowledging our self-worth, and then gives us permission to connect with our inner joy. Every parent will benefit greatly by reading Cathy's book, not only in our relationships with our children, but also in our quest to be our best selves.

GEORGIA P. DECLARK, MA, PCI
Certified Parent Coach®, preschool director/teacher

Wise and paradigm shifting, *Living What You Want Your Kids to Learn* turns traditional parenting on its head, as it invites parents to move from a "parents-know-best" approach to one in which the parent and child engage in learning and growing together. Cathy reminds us that our children are our greatest teachers— not the other way around. Our children challenge and beckon us to heal our past and return to our essential self so we can see, appreciate and support who they really are instead of cajoling, managing and manipulating them to be the 'mini-me' our ego wants them to be. With compassion and wisdom gained from her own 'wins' and mistakes as a parent, Cathy shares real-world experiences through her candid story-telling. This book is different from the hundreds of other parenting books, because instead of simply telling us how, Cathy shows us what it looks like to be a conscious parent in today's world. Warning: this book may cause miracles in your parent-child relationship. Cathy makes you want to be a better parent. If you want your relationship with your children to flourish throughout life, read this book!

RITA HYLAND
Transformational Life Coach, speaker,
Founder of Rita Hyland Coaching, LLC

I absolutely loved this book. I found myself smiling, crying, laughing and nodding in agreement as I read this beautifully written, personal collection of everyday experiences and emotions of a fellow mother genuinely trying her best to lead by example. It's easy to fall into the child-rearing trap. Keeping them on schedule, fed, bathed and on time to wherever they need to be. We don't realize that during all of these otherwise mundane activities we can be connecting with our kids on a deeper level, simply by parenting with a greater sense of self-awareness. After reading this book, I see how much my own quest for greater self-awareness is entwined with my parenting. I can grow, alongside my children, into more of the person I want to be by simply living what I'd like them to learn.

KELLY PIETRANGELI
Creator of Project Me for Busy Mothers

Cathy invites us to peek into her life as she demonstrates thought-provoking and loving anecdotes of self-aware parenting. Her personal stories are ones you can definitely relate to and each chapter will ignite your curiosity for how you can apply changes in your own life. Cathy gently reminds us that the key to connecting to our own children is in how we connect with ourselves. This isn't another parenting book—it's a personal and powerful journey into how one woman continues to practice living a life she wants her children to learn. The gift is that we're able to practice our own journey and know that we're not alone along the way. Find all these gifts and more in this book and then pass it on to another parent in your life.

JOSH BECKER
Teacher, Speaker, Author at isimply.am

LIVING
WHAT YOU WANT
YOUR KIDS TO LEARN

The Power of Self-Aware Parenting

LIVING
WHAT YOU WANT
YOUR KIDS TO LEARN

The Power of Self-Aware Parenting

CATHY CASSANI ADAMS, LCSW, CPC, CYT

Living What You Want Your Kids to Learn

The Power of Self-Aware Parenting

Cathy Cassani Adams, LCSW, CPC, CYT

F I R S T   E D I T I O N

Print ISBN: 978-1-939288-77-6

Library of Congress Control Number: 2014949253

Published by Be U

An Imprint of Wyatt-MacKenzie

To T, J, C, & S
You inspire self-awareness and joy

Kids don't remember what you try to teach them,
they remember what you are.

JIM HENSON

TABLE OF CONTENTS

LIVING WHAT YOU WANT YOUR KIDS TO LEARN
Cathy Cassani Adams, LCSW, CPC, CYT

P R A C T I C E

N O T I C E

LIVING WHAT YOU WANT YOUR KIDS TO LEARN

Cathy Cassani Adams, LCSW, CPC, CYT

ACKNOWLEDGMENTS

Thanks to my parents and my aunt who supported this book in a multitude of ways. To Tine and Drew for investing in Be U, Inc. over and over again, and to Maddie and Max for being my first self-awareness students.

To GG and Nay, thanks for the love and trust, and thanks to Monisha and Chris for the humor and comfort. You are my extended family.

Thanks to David Robert Ord for your editing expertise and guidance, and to Nancy Cleary at Wyatt-MacKenzie Publishing for supporting the message and development of this book.

Thanks to Annie Burnside for being my friend and confidant. You support me as I root and rise. You continually remind me I'm not alone. The world is better and brighter because you are in it.

Thanks to Dr. Shefali Tsabary for your trust, friendship, and support, and for bravely bringing conscious parenting into the mainstream.

To Jessica Rappè, thanks for inspiring me to question and grow. You walk the talk and demonstrate what it means to be courageous.

To Tamara O'Shaughnessy, thanks for always believing in me and creating a home for me at Chicago Parent Magazine, and to Reverend Ed Bacon for being a teacher, friend, and inspiration.

To my Dominican University students, the Be U girls and parents, and my friends in women's circle: thanks for trusting me and allowing me to share what I hold so dear.

To my beautiful ladies, Jacey, Cam, and Sky: I see you, hear you, and love you. If I were your age, I would want to be your friend. You are terrific people, and you constantly remind me to keep my heart open.

To my favorite person in the world, Todd: you are funny and kind, heart-centered and beautiful. You are my definition of home.

FOREWORD

Do you recall the part in the movie *Jerry McGuire* when Dorothy (played by Bonnie Hunt) remarks, "I'm incapable of small-talk"? Well, that's Cathy Adams. She's constantly digging for authenticity in everything she experiences. The stories in this book are drawn from those experiences.

If I had to distill Cathy's ideas down to a single expression, it would be "self-aware." Self-awareness is the starting point for everything Cathy does. After reading some of her stories, you'll find it becoming the starting point for everything you do in your roles as a parent, wife, husband, and so on.

Many of us talk a good game of being self-aware. But when the rubber meets the road, most of us fall into familiar old patterns, regardless of whether those patterns still serve us. Cathy is different in this way, in that she puts what she learns into practice.

For Cathy to integrate a new insight often requires going through quite a bit of discomfort. I know this because I've known Cathy twenty-one years and have been married to her for twelve of those. I've witnessed, and experienced these times with her.

Instead of looking outside herself for someone or something to blame for whatever may be happening, Cathy looks into the mirror and asks, "What's my role in this?" She deals with the discomfort by looking at all sides of herself, the beautiful and the ugly. It's this that makes her special.

Being married to Cathy is a wild ride. I'd like to think that, at some point, every spouse realizes there's something that makes their partner extraordinary. In Cathy's case, it's the wisdom she's gained from her own self-awareness and her desire to understand and help others.

LIVING WHAT YOU WANT YOUR KIDS TO LEARN
Cathy Cassani Adams, LCSW, CPC, CYT

You know the aisle in Barnes and Noble labeled "Self-Help"? That's Cathy's home away from home. It's a place of peace. She could spend days there and not even think about food. I'm guessing one of the places she'll want her ashes spread is in that aisle.

Another aspect of Cathy that's extraordinary is her intuition. This is a characteristic she hasn't had to develop. Instead, it's something she was born with. As I got to know her all those years ago, I noticed early on that her default mode is one of compassion and love for self and others, regardless of whether they are a family member or a beggar on the street.

One of the most important reasons I appreciate Cathy is her ability to laugh and enjoy the moment. I believe this puts her in a position to squeeze as much out of life as possible. These qualities—humor, self-awareness, and intuition—all result in a unique viewpoint, an uncommon acceptance and enjoyment of life.

In the pages ahead, you won't find techniques for how and when to give a timeout to your three-year-old, have a sex talk with your adolescent, or the best way to get your kid into an Ivy League school. What you will find are stories of how Cathy learned about herself, and life, through parenting. It's this ongoing learning that helps her constantly become a better person and parent.

Perhaps most importantly, Cathy puts our relationship, and the relationship with our kids, at the center of her world. She allows us to be her greatest teachers, and her greatest supporters. This is the foundation of self-aware parenting.

Enjoy.

TODD ADAMS
Husband and Father
Co-Founder, Be U, Inc., Co-Host Zen Parenting Radio

INTRODUCTION

I was going to be a broadcast journalist. I watched the people on the nightly news and thought their work was exciting. They had important information to share, and at the end of the day everyone tuned in to listen. I pursued this path until my second year in college.

Then one day I was sitting in a journalism class and had an out-of-the-blue epiphany: *I want to be a teacher.*

I came from a family of teachers, but until this moment it hadn't occurred to me that education was to be my path, too. Though a change in my major would mean a lot more work, specifically summer classes and eighteen credit hours a semester, I felt compelled to make the shift. So it was that I became certified in elementary education.

I graduated during an economic downturn, which meant teaching positions were limited. To find a job, I had to move to Chicago, where I was eventually hired to teach ESL and basic skills to adult students. Little did I know what this would entail. The kind of students I was assigned to needed far more than a basic education. They needed emotional support. They not only faced severe financial difficulties in many cases, but they had struggles at work and with family. I found myself listening to their experiences and offering what suggestions I could.

Listening to people in this way wasn't completely unfamiliar to me, since offering emotional support to friends and family had long felt natural to me. What I didn't realize was that all of this was preparing me for yet another shift. The more I worked with the students, the more obvious it became that I needed to go beyond teaching basic skills. I wanted to teach *life* skills.

Once again I returned to studying, this time to earn my masters in social work. Following completion of my graduate experience at Children's Memorial Hospital, I became a licensed clinical social worker. This led to an offer to serve as a clinical educator-classroom teacher in the Partial Hospitalization Program. From this foot in the door, I moved on to become a child and family therapist in child psychiatry.

A few years later, another huge shift loomed. When my first daughter was born, I made the decision to stay home with her. But without my profession, I increasingly began to feel as though I didn't know who I was. Somewhere in her first three months, I became so overwhelmed by the challenge of parenthood that I lost myself.

To try to stabilize myself, I began writing about my experiences. I also searched for a way to work from home while taking care of my baby. When I found the Parent Coaching Institute, I decided to go back to school to get my certification as a parent coach. The model resonated with me both as a professional and as a parent, focused as it was on practicing self-care, shifting attention to what's working for us, respecting a child's individuality, and practicing self-awareness. As a therapist, I can identify and diagnose a problem, while as a coach I teach introspection and attention to strengths. By balancing these two ideologies, I discovered an effective way to support parents and families.

Yoga is a physical manifestation of awareness, and for me it offers personal and professional clarity. Although the universal principles of yoga focus on seeking balance, they also stress accepting where we find ourselves right now. While yoga can be both demanding and challenging, it leads to increased openness and inner peace. For me, it's a perfect metaphor for parenting, and this guided my decision to become a yoga teacher.

When I coach, teach, present, or give yoga instruction, I send the message that life and parenting are meant to be enjoyed. Had I followed my initial intention of becoming a broadcast journalist, my daily message to my fellow humans would have likely focused on just the opposite—violence, fear, and world problems.

My choice to share a positive message isn't to deny that challenges exist. It's a question of what we focus on. Do we focus our energy on negativity, or on those things that enhance the quality of people's lives?

I take my cue from children's set point, which is one of joy. If I pay attention to them, I find they help me return to this inherent state. If I'm willing to observe and listen, they are incredible teachers.

I wonder how many of us think of our children in terms of what we can learn from them. Usually, our focus is on what we need to do for them. True, we need to keep them physically safe. They need to become acquainted with the laws and expectations of society. They require love, guidance, and nurturance in order to grow up emotionally healthy. So that they are equipped to eventually create a life of their own, they also need educating, which requires a great deal of financial support. Given the demands on us as parents to teach our children so many things, it's little wonder we overlook the fact they are here to teach us as well.

Parenting can be a phenomenal awakening experience. If one is open to it, to be a parent is like standing in front of a mirror that shows us who we are. Practicing self-awareness can be a difficult task at any age or stage of development, but as a parent it becomes especially important. Aspects of ourselves we've learned to hide, along with beliefs that don't serve us, rise to the surface. In this way, raising children draws upon our skills, while it also highlights our vulnerabilities.

The awareness that can come from parenting began exerting an impact on me shortly after I brought my first daughter home. My education and work experiences had taught me that constant productivity equals self-worth. Caring for my daughter challenged this in a hurry. Tending a baby left little time for my usual daily tasks, which rendered me unable to be productive in the way I had been in the past. Consequently I was forced to develop a different kind of confidence that was grounded not in my career, but in myself as an individual and a mother—a challenge that required a great deal of introspection, not to mention patience.

In the process of developing a new sense of my validity, I found it important to allow myself to grieve for my old life. I also did a lot of work to figure out just who I wanted to be as a parent. By testing my ability to manage crises and deal with the unknown, motherhood not only brought out aspects of me I didn't know existed, but it also altered my relationship with my spouse, my family, and my friends. This was the beginning of learning to live what I was ultimately to teach, for in due course it would become the focus of my profession.

Parenting is grounding, in that it pushes us to focus on what's most important in life, foremost of which is our relationship with others. Since it's a lifelong commitment and not something we can easily run from, it forces us to work through issues instead of shelving them in the way we often do in other relationships. The self-awareness that can come to us in this process is an amazing gift. If we take up this opportunity to grow, it offers us a path to becoming fully realized human beings.

Taking personal responsibility for our role in the parent-child relationship can be challenging, because it's much easier to focus on our children's imperfections than on the ways in which we ourselves need to grow. We'd rather close our eyes to what we bring to the relationship we create with our children. It's for this reason that parents often seek my help with what they label a "problem child." They believe that if they could only get this child to behave, the family would be just fine.

It's true that sometimes a child has behavioral issues. But the preferable course isn't to analyze the child or put them on medication, except as a last resort. Rather, a situation often resolves itself when the parents examine their interactions with the child. Parents often don't recognize the utter uniqueness of each child, which means that children give and receive love differently. The parent's job is to find the best way to reach them. A child who's acting out may be trying to communicate something beyond their ability to articulate it, which can cause them to feel unheard or unseen. When this happens, they may shut down.

Despite the fact that we love our children and have the best of intentions, we parents often focus our energy on the wrong things. For instance, we want our children to have everything we didn't have. We want them to have all the right "stuff." We also want them to take all the right classes. And, quite naturally, we like it when they say all the right things. Yet a child's needs are much simpler.

Above all else, children need to feel accepted for who they are, not just for what they do, what they say, or how they look. They need to be able to express themselves and have us listen and support them. They need our time. They require physical contact, such as holding hands or sharing a hug. They also need to feel we're taking care of ourselves, creating our own happiness, so that they don't have to shoulder this burden. It isn't the things we give them that result in a loved, confident, happy child. They just need a healthy and trusting relationship with us as their parents.

When we realize that some of our choices, with respect to our children, haven't been all that great, we may lose confidence in our parenting ability. We may experience guilt or feel shame. Quite apart from the mistakes we've made, our confidence in our parenting skills is likely to ebb and flow through the years as we are presented with more complex challenges. However, if we stay in the present instead of dwelling on past mistakes or worrying about the future, examining the experiences we are having with our children as they arise, our trust in ourselves will increase.

While guilt is the experience of knowing we made a mistake, shame is feeling we *are* a mistake. Guilt can help us learn and grow from poor choices, whereas shame will only take us down. Whenever parenting brings to the surface feelings of shame, we are being offered an opportunity to process and release outdated and unhelpful beliefs about ourselves.

As already touched on, the awareness needed to parent well begins with self-acceptance. The point of life is to learn more about who we are and grow from our experiences, which necessarily entails making mistakes. If we beat ourselves up every time we say the wrong thing or make a misstep, parenting is going to be a very difficult task. Not only does it sap our energy to be down on ourselves, but our children learn how to treat themselves based on how *we* treat ourselves. You can see how this readily becomes a vicious cycle.

Since our ability to be gentle with ourselves translates to being gentle with others, developing compassion for ourselves is one of the more important parenting skills. Our ability to be aware, own our mistakes, make appropriate changes, and continue on with grace and humility lays the foundation for our children to do the same.

Self-awareness begins with simple steps. Start by monitoring your mood when you're with your children. Are you carrying stress, resulting in your children becoming recipients of your frustration? I admit I react much differently to my children's behavior based on my mood. If I'm feeling good and they spill water, I might laugh and ask them to help me clean it up. If I'm running late or frustrated with work and they spill water, I end up giving them a lecture about being careful, then grudgingly clean it up myself. When I later reflect on the incident and realize I reacted, I can see that my children did nothing but spill water, and my mood dictated the severity of the situation.

If you are always in a hurry, assess your need to rush around and be busy. Children need activity, but they also need plenty of downtime. They require time to relax, reflect, and process—and this doesn't mean time in front of the television. Periods of stillness, imagination, play, and individual time with you are essential. If you aren't comfortable with downtime, address this issue with yourself so that your children don't have to be on your fast-paced schedule.

As I gradually shifted out of my performance-oriented mode, I discovered that downtime harbors many possibilities. It's an opportunity to give our children an extended hug that allows them to pull away when they are ready, not the perfunctory hugs we engage in when we're running to our next appointment. We can also play the game we've been promising to play for the last year, as well as actually read the books sitting on our shelf awaiting our attention. Or we might sit outside for a while or indulge in a nature walk. The key is to just be present, so that our children know we're available for their questions, and then to listen to their stories.

Slowing down and heightening your awareness may help you realize that you need a set of parenting tools, and perhaps also some support. Parenting is simultaneously the most important and the most difficult job on earth, yet so often parents feel embarrassed to ask for help or even admit they are struggling. After all, isn't being a parent supposed to be instinctive? But consider. Given that pretty much every successful CEO and great athlete has a coach or mentor, why does our society feel that parenting needs to be done in isolation?

Parents always tell me they would do just about anything for their children. Yet they often fail to take the most important step, which is to take care of themselves. It's so important to decide what you want to teach your children, then model for them the behavior you want them to learn. Make the relationship with your children and significant other your priority, which means asking for help when you need it. Don't just muddle through in isolation.

Many people look to books for guidance. Parenting books can offer a new perspective or a helpful idea, but a book shouldn't be regarded as an all-knowing guide. A book is a reference to supplement your own intuition.

While child-development books are sometimes valuable because they outline the natural stages of a child's growth and describe typical age-appropriate behavior, advice books can be confusing because they offer prescriptions that may be considered valid today but are discarded tomorrow. If you scan the shelves of parenting books, you'll see just how ever-changing and often conflicting they are. The reality is that there's no one way to parent, and ultimately you are the one who best knows your children.

I have three children, and they've taught me that I need to parent each of them a little differently. I have structure and boundaries and basic expectations, but I honor each child and each day as different. Two of my children usually get up early, whereas one likes to sleeps late. One child would rather spend time in the house, while the other two prefer to be outside. Whereas Jacey needs lots of hugs, Camryn wants to play and help me clean, and Skylar wants to hold my face and look me in the eye when she tells me stories. There's no right or wrong, only a difference in the ways they give and receive love. To parent effectively, I need to focus on their needs rather than search for a definitive answer in a book.

Sharing personal and professional stories is how I teach, which is exactly what I do in this book. One-word headings were created to attempt categorization of topics and experiences; but just as life is diverse, and our experiences far from linear, the chapters are unique and cover a mess of interactions and observations, each of which invite contemplation and consideration. Consistency lies in the practice of self-awareness, which is my constant theme, providing us as it does with the opportunity to develop a respectful and compassionate relationship with ourselves. This sets the stage for our relationship with others, which in turn unfolds as the story of our life.

Storytelling develops trust and connection, while it also normalizes common parenting experiences. A story can offer solutions, and it can equally open up a dialogue to investigate other possibilities. It allows people to contemplate their family's beliefs, which helps when it comes to making effective choices for their home.

Simply put, the key to self-aware parenting is to recognize

who you are and allow your kids to be who they are. If you want your kids to live a full life, live *your* life fully. Instead of burdening your children with your hopes and dreams for them, allow them to find their own hopes and dreams. Your children aren't an extension of you. They have their own inner world and their own path.

To parent effectively, you may need to let go of some of your old patterns, let go of needing to control, and let go of having to be right all the time. If you pay attention, your children will let you know when it's time to look at these things. For instance, they are more than willing to tell you when you're holding onto them too tightly. Children need to be held and kept safe, but they also need freedom to become who they are meant to be. It's a delicate balance that takes practice, but it's what love for our children is all about. It's what they come into our lives to teach us.

BEGINNING

For today, all you need is the grace to begin beginning.

JULIA CAMERON

1

A teenage wake-up call

WHEN I WAS SIXTEEN, I got my first speeding ticket. I ran into the house sobbing. Not only did I have a $50 fine to pay, but I also felt it wasn't fair. I told myself such things as "it wasn't my fault" and wailed "why me?"

"Maybe the police officer stopped you to keep you safe," my mother suggested, no doubt intending to soothe me. "You could have gotten in an accident down the road. Maybe this was actually a good thing."

Her words did much more than soothe me. They woke me up.

I remember it like it was yesterday—where I was, what the room smelled like, and what I was wearing. In that moment, I realized that maybe something bigger was at work—that life wasn't just about me, and that the universe was a friendly place, not "against" me. Actually, I think I *remembered* that the universe is a friendly place, because as a kid I always felt safe. I inherently sensed life worked.

Confusion had set in as I grew up because sometimes I experienced pain and saw other people in pain. I also encountered disappointment, and at times I felt afraid. Yet somehow, even though things weren't always the way I thought they should be, deep down I still somehow knew that life is good. I didn't understand how it all worked, but for some reason I trusted.

When I moved into adolescence and the teen years, my awareness of the bigger picture gradually became blurred. As my focus shifted from my internal perspective to being heavily influenced by external factors, annoying little details such as getting a speeding ticket had the ability to crush me. This simple comment by my mom that day proved to be a critical moment in which my trust in my own inner being resurfaced. Resonating with the deepest part of me, it was one of many turning points that brought me to a much fuller awareness of essentially trusting myself—a journey that has seen many bumps, lulls, and restarts.

I now know that life is meant to be enjoyed, and I understand that much of our pain and suffering comes from the kinds of things we tell ourselves. I recognize that truth comes from the heart, and I believe that love is the ultimate reality.

But more than this, I know that kids intuitively know these things. Until, that is, with the best of intentions, we inadvertently teach them differently. They learn not to trust, and they learn to listen to everyone but themselves. They also learn to be afraid.

It's important for children to be educated and to gather information, but it's more important for them to know how to live. They need to know they can trust who they are and that there's a deep part of them, which I call "inner knowing," that can serve as a compass for their life. If they follow the messages of their heart, they will know great love. Not just romantic love, but a love of self, work, friends, school, and their interests. They'll grow to love every aspect of life.

The hard part for us as parents is that our children's choices may not make sense to us. But that's because it's not *our* life. We are meant to live our own life and follow our own dreams, for it's only when we take care of ourselves that we can truly take care of others. The challenge is to live love so we can spread it around.

Just like me that day at age sixteen, we will experience disappointment. We'll also go through periods of pain, some of it perhaps excruciating. We are human, and life's ups and downs are all part of the natural way of things. But disappointment, pain, and suffering aren't our fundamental state of *being*. They are just experiences. They may also be opportunities to process an issue we haven't dealt with or learn a lesson we need to learn. As we increasingly honor these experiences instead of railing against them, we gradually return to our original self with its inherent joy, contentment, and peace of mind.

As my mother reminded me that day, the key is to not hold onto the emotions we experience at such times, but to benefit from what's happened and then let it go. Otherwise, we find ourselves predicating our lives on "what was" or "what could have been," instead of really being here.

The truth is, *here* is the only place we can ever be—it's just a matter of whether we are aware of being here or not. Making mistakes is part of how we gradually awaken to this reality, hopefully without life having to become excruciating before we at last wake up and embrace what *is*.

Comfort for the new mom

Is MOTHERHOOD THE JOYFUL experience you expected it to be, or are you overwhelmed by the whole thing? It's okay if you are. Becoming a mother is a life-altering shift, and it's actually quite normal for new mothers to feel overwhelmed.

It's surprising how people tend to tell us what we "should" be feeling as a new mother, or how "lucky" we are, while the tough times that accompany the birth of a child are a topic few are willing to talk about.

Throughout pregnancy, we expect our life to be different once the baby is born, but we don't actually know what this means until it happens. Motherhood can bring elation, guilt, tears, laughter, and a quite different perspective on things. If you are a new mom, know that the emotional swings and the sleep deprivation will eventually be under control, and that somewhere down the line you'll begin to feel comfortable with your changed reality.

People will tell you to sleep when your baby sleeps, but for some reason you feel as if you should fold the laundry and write thank-you notes. People might offer to watch your baby for an hour or two, but you decline the offer because you're concerned about germs or the possibility of a kidnapper breaking in while you are absent. Such concerns are typical in the early days of motherhood.

However, it's important to ask for and accept appropriate help when it's offered. Keep in mind that if you take care of yourself, you can better care for your baby. To be a person who can make rational choices for this helpless human being, you need sufficient rest to supply the energy you require. Playing the part of a martyr by doing it all alone can lead to a feeling of isolation and ultimately, resentment.

The day I exploded when my husband said he was going to Target, it became clear I needed time away from our first baby. I said, "You're going to Target? I don't get to just *go* to Target anymore. I have to plan to go to Target. You're free to go to Target anytime you want, and I'm trapped!" As a result of this outburst, my husband and I both realized I desperately needed time to myself.

The foundation of your family is you and your partner. For things in the home to run smoothly, this foundation needs to be strong. Bringing a new baby into the family will necessitate a lot of communication, and don't be surprised if there are breakdowns in communication at times.

You can help things by making it a goal to share your feelings with your partner, no matter what they may be, so that you can work as a team. Taking care of yourself in this way will help alleviate your desire to lash out at him when he's showered and rested, but you aren't.

As the way you live and how you think change in response to having a baby in the house, embrace the different person you are becoming. Have confidence that what your role as a parent demands of you is something that, in time, you will become clearer about and more comfortable with.

To help in this process, perhaps find a moms' group in which you can share your frustrations and listen to the experiences of others. Talk with friends about their early mothering experiences so they can assure you that things will calm down.

As a mother, your heart naturally becomes bigger. Not just for your child, but for the world. This is because you realize that everybody is someone's child, and everybody was once as innocent as your baby.

As you notice more, feel more, and worry more, you also develop greater compassion, more patience, and true gratefulness. You learn what love means in practice. You realize that although the reality of motherhood may not be exactly what you expected, this doesn't make it any less amazing.

3

Measuring worth through productivity

As a working woman, I had a title, an office, and a purpose. My worth was measured by my productivity. Completing tasks and attaining goals was the essence of my existence. I experienced a sense of accomplishment at the end of the day, and I felt worthy of my paycheck and my weekends. I believed my education and previous work experiences had led me to this point, for I had become who I set out to be and felt I knew who I was.

When I became a mother, I experienced an identity crisis. I had no experience of being a mother and felt extremely insecure in the face of the day-to-day challenges of parenting. Even if I created a list of tasks, it was almost impossible to cross things off since my time was no longer my own. Being a mother was devoid of predictability, and there was no way to measure my productivity.

When 6:00 p.m. rolled around, I often wondered what I had done all day. All I knew was that I was getting by on five hours of interrupted sleep and I had kept my baby fed, diapered, and nurtured. Was that really all I had to show for myself?

Though I had stacks of parenting books all over the house and constantly called more-experienced mothers in a bid to alleviate my anxiety, I had to admit I was a complete novice.

It was as if, after a successful career, I had started over.

Accomplishing things has always been important to me. Consequently, even when I was experiencing beautiful moments with my baby, my thoughts drifted to her naptime when I could at last get something done. In fact, it often felt like I was merely going through the motions when I spent time with my baby, the aim being to have more valuable time with my computer and my checklist. After all, this was how I'd always measured my effectiveness.

While my baby slept, I tackled the tasks I deemed most important, crossing off my list whatever I could. I loved the natural high of getting things accomplished—though, like a drug, it was never enough, and I always felt that I should have done more. The truth is, I was quite detached from my new life because I was measuring my value in a way that simply didn't work for my changed situation. As a result, I no longer knew who I was or had a sense of my importance.

As time passed, I began to embrace the distinct difference between a career and parenting. At work, efficiency and productivity are what count, whereas to be a good mom requires us to slow down, become present in each moment, and not only be physically present with our child but also emotionally available.

In this changed situation, our worth is no longer measured by completed tasks or how busy we are. Instead, it's measured by picking up a child when she cries, enjoying conversation during dinner, and explaining why eating play dough is yucky.

As I slowly became aware that my children were meant to be my teachers, I attempted to experience their world when we were together. As I did so, I began to understand that children only live in the present, and they have all the time in the world. For them every little thing is exciting, and there's always something to learn even from a story they've heard many times. They choose the same books to be read to them over and over. Building a tower and knocking it down is much more fun the tenth time. And they just love unfolding freshly folded laundry.

At times my mind still drifts to time on my computer, but now I notice such thoughts and question their validity. I may be unconsciously pulled toward tasks and lists, but I recognize they aren't more important; they are just more ingrained. Feeding, bathing, and putting my kids to bed can at times seem monotonous, while it can also generate feelings of worth and deep connection if I stay present with what I'm doing.

Making the choice to slow down with my child has been a major shift from my previous life, and I may always be a work in progress on this score. But even though parenthood as a whole isn't a task I can "complete," I hope to stay present enough to appreciate it. I already know I will one day reflect fondly on these often mundane tasks. When the time comes that such tasks are no longer needed, I already know they'll be missed.

4

Practicing self-care

I OFTEN HEAR PARENTS say they feel they are "losing themselves" to parenthood, to the point that their life is becoming a blur. If this is happening to you, I want you to know that it's a choice, not an absolute.

We lose ourselves to parenthood when we put everyone's needs ahead of our own. Life becomes a blur because we don't take time to think, plan, learn, and experience gratitude. If we are constantly giving of our time, energy, and love, without taking time to refuel, we'll inevitably become drained.

Self-care is personal, which is why it means something different to everybody. One person enjoys thirty minutes of time alone in the mornings, while another needs a morning jog. Some of us need time with friends. For others of us, weekly dates with a partner are essential. And for still others, time to be creative is what we value.

So, how you can best take care of yourself? Well, you might start with the following questions:

- What gives me energy?
- Who gives me energy?
- When do I feel calm and centered?
- When do I feel fulfilled?

- How can I use my talents and my skills?
- How can I become more aware, so that I appreciate the gifts in my life?

As parents, we inhabit a different reality from that of others. We may not be able to do everything we want, whenever we want to do it. The trick is to figure out how to incorporate what we desire into our existing situation. To this end, here are some factors worth pondering:

- How can I incorporate these things into my life?
- How can I be realistic about these expectations?
- What do I want my life to look and feel like?
- Who will support me? Who will help me?

I find it helps to have some kind of vision of where I'm headed. Once this is in place, finding a support network may be important for you, depending on your particular makeup. Not only can it help many of us when it comes to implementing our vision, but it can also keep us on track. As I mentioned earlier, at the very least we need people who will assist with basics like babysitting.

The shifts we are undergoing have an impact on a wider front, since whenever we take care of ourselves, it tends to benefit the people around us. For this reason, once we take action and implement our plan, it's worth noting how we feel when we make ourselves a priority. You might ask yourself such questions as: Are my children seeing me smile more? Am I being kinder to my significant other? One of the best gifts we can give our family is to bring contentment into the home.

It's also important that our relationships with our friends continue developing. One of my many self-care practices is to spend special time with my girlfriends at least once a month. When this day rolls around, I make a point to tell my daughters how excited I am to spend time with my friends. I tell them the names of all of my friends and I show them pictures. This usually initiates a wonderful conversation about my daughters' playmates and friends. As I leave the house, my children give me a hug and wave to me with a smile.

Witnessing my self-care teaches my daughters the importance of self-love in the form of friendship. They also see that Mom has even more energy to share with them when she returns.

ACCEPTANCE

Grant me the serenity to accept the things I cannot change;
courage to change the things I can;
and wisdom to know the difference.

SERENITY PRAYER

A miscarriage

FOR SOME REASON I TOOK the girls to my appointment. Though I've attended many doctor appointments over the years, it had never occurred to me to bring the girls. I guess that normally I thought I should go alone, other than those occasions when my husband would accompany me just in case something was wrong. But this was my third pregnancy, and I had seen this baby's heartbeat.

For some, the number of children they have is a simple decision, but I was uncertain how many I wanted. I came from a family of two, and my sister had a family of two, so three didn't feel familiar. In fact, it felt chaotic. How could I handle a family of three?

Because I was 35, I was also afraid to try for a third child. Once you're 35 or more, you're made to believe a pregnancy is risky. I was so fearful, the idea of having another child made me as dizzy as the thought of not having another child.

At the same time, I felt a longing. Honoring my need to process these emotions and reach a decision that had been well thought out, I spent over a year and half deciding whether or not our family was ready for this addition.

After counseling, praying, and time spent in much-needed

silence, I realized someone was missing from this family. The awareness dawned in me that, deep down, I wanted another child. Making the decision was not only exciting but also liberating, because I broke through an entrenched pattern of thinking and cleared out the useless fear that was part of this pattern. So when I was ready to move forward, I took a leap of faith and stepped into the unknown.

The doctor entered, said hello to my girls, and asked how I felt. I was able to report that although I had been desperately sick from weeks six to ten, thankfully my symptoms had magically disappeared. I attributed this to a few acupuncture appointments and a necessary attitude adjustment. "I made myself better," I said proudly.

I could instantly tell the doctor wasn't happy with this news. "Do you have any other symptoms of pregnancy?" she asked. As I sensed concern, my heart leapt into my throat. I had never had a disagreeable doctor's appointment, and I had certainly never seen this look on a doctor's face.

As the doctor reached for the Doppler to locate my baby's heartbeat, I felt myself shift into a world of slow motion. I watched as she moved the instrument around my stomach, and it began to dawn on me that she couldn't find a heartbeat. As if in a dream, I slowly sat up, saying as I did so, "You can't find it, can you?"

Feeling the tension in the air, my daughters were calm, quiet.

On my way to the hospital for an ultrasound, I called to try to find my sister so that she could watch the girls. When I also called my husband, who was driving home from a work trip, I realized I was going to go through this experience alone. He assured me everything was fine, and that the ultrasound would confirm our baby was healthy. After all, the doctor did say that sometimes eleven weeks is too early to pick up a heartbeat on a Doppler.

Intuition has long been a vital component of how I function, but at that moment my intuitive abilities were nowhere in sight. I didn't know what to believe. The one thing I knew was that I had gone through too much for this pregnancy not to progress. The process of deciding whether or not to have a third child had been such a spiritual awakening that it had become the beginning a whole new chapter of my life. "This child is supposed to come," I reassured myself.

"Let's hope for the best," said the hospital technician, gently supporting my head as I lay down for the ultrasound. Observing her face rather than watching the screen, I saw her shake her head. The news wasn't good. Slowly moving my eyes toward the computer screen, I saw my tiny, tiny baby and could tell immediately that this child wasn't alive. There was no movement, no vitality.

The image of my baby on the screen is forever etched in my mind.

I vaguely remember the technician telling me that the baby only measured at nine weeks. This meant my morning sickness had ceased not as a result of my efforts, but because this pregnancy had come to an end.

I let out a loud gasp, as if somebody had just hit me. And I cried, a deep and painful cry, at the thought that there was no way I could hold my baby, kiss it, soothe it.

The grief was devastating. Each of the doctors and nurses reassured me this wasn't my fault, though I can't help looking back and wondering what I might have done differently.

As the days passed, I was astounded at the number of

women who shared with me that they too had suffered a miscarriage. From family members and close friends, to the surgical nurse who held my hand through the D&C, I felt a deep collective ache.

Weeks passed, and I was unsure of what to do next. I realized I had already been blessed with two children. How lucky I was to have my daughters. Now, when I looked at them, I realized more than ever how much they meant to me.

People have told me it's worse to miscarry a first pregnancy, since there's a greater sense of hopelessness. Though this is undoubtedly true, knowing it did nothing to alleviate my sadness. As the grief and accompanying anger washed over me, I had to somehow find a way to accept my loss and hold onto my belief that I would find a new normal.

But for now, I just missed my baby. I missed what could have been.

I explained to my daughters that the baby we had loved and talked so much about had stopped growing and wouldn't be coming. My three-year-old hugged my stomach and asked softly, "Maybe another baby will come?"

With hope, but undeniable uncertainty, I could only answer, "Maybe."

6

Pregnant again—stepping into the unknown

ALTHOUGH I GRIEVED LONG and experienced paralyzing ambivalence following my miscarriage, somewhere along the way I again stepped into the unknown.

I wanted to do it differently this time. I didn't want to live in fear, but to enjoy each moment of the experience.

To eliminate unnecessary stress from this pregnancy, I gave away all my books about pregnancy—all that information about how awful I was going to feel, and what to "watch out for" each month. Instead, I chose books that describe pregnancy as a time of joy and childbirth as a healthy, normal process. Pregnancy, and the birth I felt confident it would result in, became my new adventure.

Rather than recommending that women avoid pain through medical intervention, the books I now read suggested becoming mentally and physically prepared for the labor experience. Natural birth, they assured me, is a rite of passage, a psycho-spiritual training ground for mother and child. They extolled the health benefits for both mother and baby, as well as the bond that forms during the birth process. This was something I wanted to experience.

My older daughters had been born with the help of an

epidural in a traditional hospital setting, so I decided that this time I wanted a place that supported a more natural experience. I found an alternative birthing center and a midwife practice. I enlisted the help of a good friend who is a Bradley instructor and my parent coach, who also happens to be a birth doula. (In case you aren't familiar with the term "doula," it refers to is a nonmedical person, who may or may not be certified, who provides physical and emotional support for a woman before, during, and after childbirth, along with assisting her partner and family.)

Together, my support team taught me about the birth experience and provided me with tools to help with pregnancy and delivery. Though natural birth was the goal, they also stressed that I needed to be open to whatever might unfold, since it's impossible to be in full control of pregnancy and birth. As we talked through my fears, they consistently empowered me. Surrounding myself with women who believed I could do this was tremendously reassuring.

Since this adventure wasn't just for me, but for my whole family, my husband became my birth partner, and my daughters attended my monthly appointments. The midwives encouraged me to bring the girls into the room so that they could hear the heartbeat of their new sibling. They helped by holding my hand, and sometimes even by guiding the Doppler.

As the months went by, I not only felt increasingly confident, but I also found myself becoming strong. My mind was grounded, my energy good. My body felt great, and the normal aches and pains were minor. I also felt more effective as a mother and a partner.

Another benefit of my pregnancy was the positive effect it had on my career as a coach. My boundaries were expanding, which meant I was open to taking more risks as a professional. I shared more of my writing, made myself available for interviews, and gave more presentations.

When my due date drew near, I felt ready. I had studied visualization and relaxation techniques, along with walking and doing yoga daily. It was like training for a marathon. Then as the due date came and went, I was initially frustrated—though I soon found myself amused by the obvious lesson coming my way. Patience and giving up control are essential when you become a parent. My daughters had taught me this, and this baby was refreshing my memory.

Eight days past my due date, I awakened during the night with contractions, excited to put my new tools to good use. Though I fully experienced the tremendous challenge of labor, I continued to trust that the baby knew exactly what to do.

As we drove to the birthing center in the middle of the night, running red lights, I lay on the floor of our minivan and realized the baby wasn't going to wait. I yelled to my husband to let him know I was about to give birth. I had no choice but to push. By the time we pulled up to the emergency room, the baby's head was out. No one believed me, instead insisting that I sit in a wheelchair. I insisted that I needed to walk into the ER and immediately lie down. Moments later, my third daughter was born.

The whirlwind process was unlike anything I could have anticipated, although it was exactly the way it was supposed to be. I never expected or planned for a perfect birth. I just wanted to be alert so I could fully participate. I felt open to, and prepared for, whatever might unfold. What came was a great story to tell for years to come.

I understand and respect that there are different ways to

ACCEPTANCE
Cathy Cassani Adams, LCSW, CPC, CYT

birth a child. I'm surrounded by loved ones who required medical intervention during both pregnancy and labor, and I'm humbled by the skilled specialists and technology that helped their children come into the world.

For me, however, this journey wasn't simply about experiencing a natural birth, but was an opportunity to discover more about myself and what I'm capable of. Through the experience, I learned that instead of talking so much about the potential negatives, women need to emphasize to each other the positive possibilities.

The lesson that I don't control outcomes, and therefore need to be more open and fluid in my expectations, is one of the reasons we named our new little girl Skylar. She symbolizes expansiveness. I'm excited to pass this learning experience on to all of my daughters. I feel a responsibility to raise my girls to be free of unnecessary limitations.

In sharing my experience, I want to honor all of my children, but especially my third child, the pregnancy I lost at eleven weeks. It was because of you that I decided to go deeper and discover a new path. Thank you for pointing out the direction I needed to go.

Saying goodbye to the pacifier

WHEN MY DAUGHTER WAS BORN, she took to the pacifier immediately. It soothed her in every situation—restaurants, the middle of the night, between feedings, on an airplane. It was her solace, so we made sure we carried it everywhere.

As she grew up, her love affair with the "paci," as she calls it, continued. The need for one paci increased to two—one for her mouth and one for her hand, just in case. The paci offered immediate comfort, soothing her not only when she fell but also when she felt misunderstood.

As we approached the age when most children give up the pacifier—usually because the parents feel it's the right time—we talked with our daughter about letting it go. With great conviction, she announced she wasn't ready.

When we allowed her to keep it, caring friends remarked, "It only gets harder." Others warned us about the "danger" to her teeth. We realized this advice was given with the best of intentions, but we were unwilling to take the pacifier away without our daughter participating in the decision-making. Not wishing the soothing she experienced in body and mind to come to an abrupt halt, we elected to wean her off it slowly.

ACCEPTANCE
Cathy Cassani Adams, LCSW, CPC, CYT

We began the process by setting some boundaries around her use of the pacifier. Though she was welcome to use it, she had to be in her room. Later, we decided it was only to be used before naptime or bedtime. Handling these subtle transitions with ease, she began exploring different ways to soothe herself during the day—though at night she still looked forward to the comfort of the paci.

On her birthday, we gave her a bag with four pacifiers, explaining that these would be the "final four." She was responsible for them, and she would decide when to give them up. Together we brainstormed four celebrations, one for each pacifier. For the first, we would go to the library. For the second, she could pick her favorite restaurant for dinner. For the third, she would buy a book at the bookstore. And for the fourth, we planned a "paci party" with dinner, cake, and a movie.

She gave up the first pacifier immediately, handing it over without a second thought. We headed to the library. A week later, she handed over the second pacifier, and we had a wonderful dinner that evening, replete with toasts to her growth and new beginnings. Two days later, the third pacifier also bit the dust. In the bookstore, she chose a book about a princess.

Then came the big lull. The fourth pacifier was staying put! A few times when it got lost, we explained she would have to find it on her own, since we had clearly told her it was entirely her responsibility. Full of compassion, we explained that maybe it knew it was time to go. Each time she lost it, she searched frantically, and it would always turn up. I think we thought the pacifier would eventually develop a hole, but she learned to put it in its bag every morning. Though it came out for an occasional cleaning, it otherwise remained safe. She held onto it for a significant period, taking responsibility for it almost like a pet. It wasn't always in her mouth at night—she held it a lot.

The day came when we decided she needed some encouragement, so we told her it was time to start planning the paci party. Pulling out a calendar, we let her pick a date that felt right to her. Then, the day of the paci party, we presented her with a little pillow with her name on it. We sat together, and each member of the family hugged the pillow and "put our love into it" so that she could have us with her while she slept. Family members sent cards of encouragement and support, and we read them aloud.

After a wonderful evening of celebration, it was time to go to bed. As she lay on her bed with the paci in her mouth, I could see her brain churning. She had treasured this little piece of serenity ever since the day she had come home from the hospital, but now it was time for her to say goodbye. Looking at me, she placed it in my hand.

As I hugged her, I felt her shake. Backing up, intending to dry her tears, I realized she was laughing. Her eyes were bright, and she appeared proud and confident. We tucked her in with her new pillow and said goodnight, and she fell asleep with a smile on her face.

The only person who cried that night was me. As I threw that pink pacifier into the garbage, I thanked it for soothing my daughter and allowing her to go within and calm herself. I thanked it for all the uninterrupted dinners at restaurants, the peaceful nights, and the plane rides when her ears were popping. I felt great appreciation for its role in my daughter's life, and I'm glad she was able to let it go in such a positive way.

Goodbye, old friend.

ACCEPTANCE
Cathy Cassani Adams, LCSW, CPC, CYT

8

My daughter didn't have to dance

THE DRESS REHEARSAL WENT GREAT. Even getting ready for the rehearsal went well.

My daughter Camryn is usually sensitive to tags and tight-fitting clothing, but she was all smiles as she put on her costume for the dress rehearsal for the dance recital. Though the tights she was required to wear were thick, she pulled them up without any show of frustration. Her hat needed several bobby pins, but she didn't even flinch when I put them in. The whole evening flowed flawlessly, which generated even more excitement for the actual performance.

On the big night, we arrived an hour early, which meant a lot of waiting around. It was hot. The dressing rooms and hall-ways were filled with people charged with energy. Boys and girls of all ages were putting on makeup and running around in their costumes. My four-year-old dancer was taking in every moment.

About ten minutes before the show, parents were asked to take their seats in the auditorium. Camryn stood with her dance group and supervisor, waving to me as I left to find my seat with the rest of our family. After enjoying the opening numbers,

I glanced at the program and noticed that Camryn's performance was only minutes away.

Just then I felt a tap on my shoulder and heard someone say, "Mrs. Adams, Camryn is having a meltdown in the hallway." Handing my one-year-old to my husband, I bolted from my seat.

Camryn was surrounded by girls from her class, together with several well-meaning moms. Seeing me, she began crying even louder. As I picked her up, she grabbed onto my neck with all her strength. After a minute or so of silence, I asked her what was wrong. Maintaining her grip, she shook her head.

By now her class was lining up. It was time for them to go backstage. "Are you going to dance tonight?" I asked her in a gentle voice. Again she shook her head telling me no. Making eye contact with her teacher, I said, "I don't think Camryn is going to make it tonight."

"Tell her you'll buy her something if she gets out there," the teacher suggested.

One of the moms also chimed in, "Tell her that she *needs* to go out there. Tell her she'll love it."

I heard their words, though I also knew such suggestions would prove ineffective. Right now, Camryn couldn't see beyond the present moment. Besides, I knew it wasn't right for me to bribe her or tell her what she ought to be feeling.

As the dance group moved backstage, I slowly followed, with Camryn clinging to me. Observing "oh-no" looks from moms and the stagehand, who seemed particularly frustrated that the situation hadn't been resolved, I eased Camryn away from my body and coaxed, "Honey, you can dance for a few minutes with your friends, then come back and sit with me. I'll stay here and watch you."

ACCEPTANCE

Cathy Cassani Adams, LCSW, CPC, CYT

Camryn shook her head and again fastened her hands around my neck. Shaking my head to let the other parents know she wasn't going to participate, I closed my eyes. It was then that I realized it was time for me to let go. With the preceding dance number now over, Camryn's class were taking hold of each other's hands, ready to go on stage.

Drawing a deep breath, I thought about what was happening. *This feels big right now,* I told myself, *but in the big picture it isn't important.*

The truth was Camryn had loved every dance class for the last six months. She was never motivated by this big moment, but instead enjoyed the whole process. She was thrilled about her costume and getting made up. She was also excited to see her grandparents and have dinner with them before the show. Having enjoyed every aspect of this opportunity, not dancing tonight would in no way detract from these experiences. I smiled, rested my head against her head, and allowed these encouraging insights to float through my mind.

Suddenly Camryn sniffed, looked at me, and let go of my neck. Jumping down, she joined hands with a girl from her class and they walked on stage, where she took her place under the lights and performed through sniffs and smiles. Her performance turned out to be even more enthusiastic than the rehearsal. I was dumbfounded. Peering through the curtain, I felt dizzy. How did we get from there to here?

A mom placed her hand on my shoulder and asked, "What did you say to her?"

I shook my head and explained that I had said nothing, but that Camryn simply changed her mind. With this realization, I found myself tearing up, both relieved and simultaneously overwhelmed by the emotion of the moment.

After the recital, we decided to celebrate by going out for ice cream. Alone with Camryn at a table, I asked her, "Can you tell me what you were feeling right before your performance?"

She looked at me and said, "I was just afraid I would get lost."

I sat back in my chair, thinking to myself, *Aren't we all?*

Camryn may have been referring to getting lost like she did at the museum the week before. Or perhaps she felt lost because the energy around her was so high. She may even have felt lost because her mom seemed far away in the auditorium. It could also have simply been stage fright at the thought of appearing before a sold-out auditorium. Whatever the reason, I nodded to her and assured her I understood.

"We all feel lost sometimes, even big people," I explained. Then I told her how proud I was that she decided to walk onstage even though she was experiencing such strong feelings. As I did so, I again found myself tearing up, moved by her honesty and self-understanding.

I too sometimes feel lost as an individual, a parent, and a professional. I have moments of uncertainty and fear. I question whether I'm good enough. I also wonder if I'll lose my way. Such uncertainties creep in when I least expect them—which is why I cherish this new set of coping skills from my daughter.

Feel your feelings, grab the hands of the people around you, step under the lights, and dance with bravery and joy.

Accepting my headaches

EVERY COUPLE OF MONTHS I get a big headache, so big that it sidelines me at least for a day. These headaches are unwelcome, and I wouldn't wish them on anyone. Though in hindsight, I have to confess that they are amazing teachers.

When I'm feeling good, unfortunately all I tend to notice is what I could have done better, done more of, and should have said differently—all of which is such an energy drain. Headaches remind me to be grateful when I feel good, as well as to be pleased with the effort I put out each day instead of dwelling on the ways in which I fall short.

Because I dwell too much on the undone rather than the done, these headaches always take me back to basics, causing me to ponder how I spend my day and whether it's what I really want to be doing. I examine what I focus on and how I use my energy. Lying in bed, I have a clear sense of what I do every day. I recognize the effort I put into my schedule and the sincerity I invest in my parenting. I feel admiration for the way I maintain my busy schedule.

When I'm lying in bed, I also hear my children downstairs. I love their stories and their energetic voices. I listen to them from afar without needing to teach. I appreciate them without needing to respond to them. Even though they are just a floor below me, I miss them and miss our interaction. I guess you could say that pain and the inability to do things brings everything into sharp focus.

Although I'm speaking of headaches, I've also felt this way when confronted with the illness of a parent or my child, not to mention when I have to stop and feel the challenges of life.

The message is always the same, however. Notice what's here. Appreciate what you have. Stop thinking you need to be more than who you are, or that you need to do more than you're already doing. Look out the window and notice the day. Listen to your children's voices, hug your husband, feel what it feels like to be present in this moment.

While I'm thankful for this teaching, I wish I could integrate the understanding into my everyday awareness. I wish it didn't take headaches to make me understand what really matters in life.

Oh, there I go again, thinking I should be better than I am.

10

Teach body acceptance by accepting your body

TEACHING OUR CHILDREN not only to accept but also honor their bodies is a vital task for parents. Unfortunately, our attempts to do this are often overshadowed by the way we talk about *ourselves*.

Many of us dislike the way we look and even express hatred for parts of our body. All the while, our children are watching and listening as we attack ourselves. They don't hear us say we love our bodies. They don't see us embrace ourselves in a loving way.

Many of us have an especially conflicted relationship with food. Obsessed with weight management, we base our self-worth on a scale. We feel good about losing five pounds, then feel bad about gaining two. We demonstrate how a number can dictate our mood, choices, and self-worth. As our children listen to us criticizing our looks, they also watch as we treat food like an enemy. Instead of learning from us how food can help our bodies move and grow, they see us focus solely on how it affects our appearance. They observe how we try every diet, restrict what we eat, or overeat and feel guilty. Thus they learn to fight with food rather than enjoy it.

We can blame television and magazines with their super-skinny models, but we perpetuate being judged by judging ourselves on a daily basis. Although we can't control the media, we can make a choice not to degrade ourselves when we try on clothes, let alone cringe whenever we pass a mirror. We can practice noticing how well our body actually works—how miraculously it functions and moves.

We can also begin to appreciate food for the simple reason that we always have access to it. We can begin to see food as a gift to our body and senses.

I recognize that weight and body image can be issues, and I know that countless factors contribute to these issues. But I'm also acutely aware that I'm raising three girls, and that they watch me closely. For them, I can choose to be aware of what I say and practice treating myself kindly, especially in their presence. I can choose to talk about being grateful for the way my body moves, and I can express how much I appreciate a great meal.

I can also tell my daughters how much I appreciate my comfy shirt or how I enjoy the feel of a long, flowing skirt. And in the mornings, as they watch me get ready for the day, I can look at myself in the mirror and smile.

This isn't always easy. Like most people, I have my own baggage when it comes to body image. But each time I practice loving behavior toward myself, I find it healing. Instead of struggling to be different, I begin to understand what it means to "love what is."

I can't completely shield my daughters from the pressure of our society; they may experience their own issues with body acceptance. But while they are young, I can model some alternatives, thereby equipping them with tools that can nurture their growing sense of self—such as the ability to appreciate the way their body moves, the joy of a great meal, or the feel of a comfy skirt.

Or the desire to catch a glimpse of themselves in a mirror and smile.

11

The problem with no right answers and needing to be right

THERE WAS A TIME WHEN I ate whatever food was in the store, did whatever my doctor told me to do, and watched television with no concern for my mental well-being. Now I have to worry about what I'm eating. Are the vegetables organic? If they are organic, have they been washed? And if I wash them, is the water I use full of chemicals?

These days I don't have one healthcare practitioner; I have several, both medical and holistic, who each offer me differing opinions. I hear statements such as "dairy is essential," and the reverse, "dairy is bad for you." I'm told vaccines are beneficial, while someone else insists vaccines are harmful. A particular medicine is going to help me, one expert assures me, whereas another says the medicine won't help at all and may even do damage.

Also, technology that was created to assist us has in some ways made our lives more complex, taking over our time, affecting our ability to communicate, leaving us to decide how much is too much—not just for ourselves, but also for our children.

ACCEPTANCE
Cathy Cassani Adams, LCSW, CPC, CYT

Such things are merely the tip of the iceberg when it comes to all the situations we have to consider on a daily basis. It's difficult to know who's the expert and truly interested in our well-being. It leaves us feeling alone, vulnerable, unsure about our choices. And we wonder why we feel anxious.

It's of little surprise that we become defensive when anyone questions our decision-making. To advocate for ourselves and our family is overwhelming, so extensive is the information thrown at us on a daily basis.

We live in an era of diverse perspectives, in a world that's constantly changing, which means there are no easy answers. All we can do is make the best choice we know for this moment right now. It's unwise to plan too far ahead, and it certainly isn't helpful to hold onto past mistakes. We have to embrace our own present-moment clarity, making the best game-time decisions we know to make with the information we have at present.

The fact that we live in the information age doesn't make it any less essential to tap into our ability to "feel" what's right for us. We can read everything under the sun, but in the end there will still be a dozen different kinds of coconut oil on the shelf. How do we know which to choose? We have to tap into our gut muscle, trust ourselves, and roll with it. We also need to be sufficiently fluid to realize we may come back another time for a different coconut oil. But today, right now, this is our best choice.

The real issue is our *anxiety* about doing everything correctly. Such anxiety is epidemic. But why be anxious, when there's absolutely no way to do everything right all the time? It's impossible to be on top of everything. We are going to make mistakes.

While I practice due diligence when it comes to choosing

the best coconut oil, or anything else for that matter, I'm also learning to be flexible in my choices. I'm letting go of the need to be right all the time, instead trusting what feels right in the moment. My choices may not be perfect, but they are choices that allow me to smile during the day and sleep at night.

Maybe instead of needing to have all the information, needing to be right, we can become present-day experiencers and open-minded learners. We will at least be more forgiving of ourselves, as well as more understanding and compassionate when others make mistakes.

Maybe we will begin to understand that there is no one way. There is only this day, this moment, and this choice right now.

ACCEPTANCE
Cathy Cassani Adams, LCSW, CPC, CYT

Responding to criticism

THE MOST COMMON CRITICISM of my writing and radio show is, "You need to talk more about your problems, be more real." I know what people are trying to say, but the truth is that, at 43, I *am* finally being real.

When something happens, I don't see only what's in front of me. I see the whole picture, which includes why it might have happened and how it relates to the bigger picture. I like to think of it as a wide-angle lens. Because of my application of this lens, I don't see situations or people as inherently bad. I see how things fit together or didn't fit together to create the situation.

When I was young, I was one of those kids who spins in a field of flowers, looking up to the sky, thinking about how life is good. At least, that's my perception of how I was back then. But people, formal education, and my experiences have caused me to question my perspective. In my life I have been called naïve, unintelligent, unsavvy, uneducated, unaware, and disconnected from reality. Basically, people wanted me to wake up and notice that life sucks.

Maybe I needed to acknowledge a bigger picture. We all need balance. But viewing life in this way, seeing it through a lens of fear and obstacles, actually *caused* me to feel unaware and disconnected. It *caused* me to lose my way, so I was left feeling confused and depressed.

Many years ago, I began working my way back to the spinning kid in the field, as it slowly dawned on me that being born as her was my life's gift. I suck at many things—math, directions, reading manuals, understanding technology, board games, taking tests, staying organized, understanding fashion, and drawing. In addition to such things, I'm most sad that I can neither sing nor tap dance. I always wanted to have a great singing voice, always wanted to dance and be Madonna.

Though I suck at so many things, I was born with my wide-angle lense—born looking up at the sky. I see good stuff everywhere, feel good stuff in people. When someone asks me a deep question, information just pours into my head. Some of it comes from experience, some of it from my formal education. Then there's the part that just comes to me, though I have no idea where it comes from. When I'm in this mode, I can write something one day and not recognize it the next.

I spent a lot of my years pushing my gift away, thinking I was stupid or missing something others seemed to understand. Now I get it. Like all humans, pain, crisis, fear, and sadness are part of my life experience. The truth is, I feel these things deeply, sometimes too deeply. Often I feel other people's stuff deeply, though it has nothing to do with me.

Mine has been a hard-fought battle to balance what I can feel with what I can control. Most things I can't control, so I practice letting go. I cry a lot. I take a lot of baths and showers. I sit in quietude and breathe.

Living life is a practice, and I'm getting better at it. I can now walk through the world without feeling exposed to the ele-

ACCEPTANCE
Cathy Cassani Adams, LCSW, CPC, CYT

ments. I can have deep talks with others without feeling I've been hit by a ton of bricks. Even more importantly, I'm brave enough to use my real voice again—the one I used to hear in my head as a kid. I get to talk about love, compassion, and joy with my kids, my husband, my friends. I get to do what comes naturally to me for a living.

So when someone tells me to talk more about life's difficulties, or when they inform me other people see the world differently, it reminds me that it can be difficult to be "seen." I do face challenges, and I share these challenges with the people I know and love—those who have demonstrated an ability to listen and empathize. What I share in my blogs and on the show, and now in this book, is what I've come to understand based on those challenges.

If there's a single theme to my recent years, it's that I've become more fully myself. I hear you when you say you want me to talk more about my problems; but if I did, I would be doing it for other people's comfort. For me, that's a step backward. Being myself through writing, talking, and teaching are the ways I sing and dance—the ways I use my gifts to be of service and feel good.

It's just me, spinning in the fields.

INSPIRATION

Start by doing what's necessary; then do what's possible; and suddenly you are doing the impossible.

FRANCIS OF ASSISI

Anything is possible

CAMRYN, FIVE YEARS OLD: "Mom, is anything possible?"

Me: "Absolutely."

Camryn: "But crayons can't fly."

Me: "Why not?"

Camryn: "I don't know."

Ten minutes later, Camryn: "What if I draw a crayon, then cut it out and hold it in front of the fan. Then it will fly through the air!"

Me: "Sounds like crayons can fly."

Camryn: "I'm so glad anything is possible."

Me: "Me, too."

Children inspire me. They view life with an open mind and creative spirit. They also exude a feeling of confidence, a belief in who they are and what they can do. This is how they come into the world.

At one time we were all this way. We believed in ourselves, knew who we were, and allowed our heart to guide us. But the way we were parented, the formal education we received, and any number of experiences that happened to us taught us to doubt ourselves. We learned to look to others for answers, to be like them, and to fulfill their hopes and dreams for us.

This shutting down of who we intrinsically are isn't done maliciously but out of a concern for our well-being. Who doesn't want their children to fit in? Who doesn't want them to be accepted by society? The problem is that blending in and being like everyone else causes children to lose touch with their true self—their individuality, creativity, and unique way of expressing themselves.

At some point in our lives, we may decide it's time to get back in touch with our original way of being. Such may be triggered by feeling an emptiness or detachment from our everyday experiences, even if our life on paper looks pretty good. Something within us nags at us to figure out who we were before we worked so hard to blend in. It's now that we seek to quiet the running tape of "shoulds" in our head so that we can listen to what we really want for our lives.

When awareness of dissatisfaction first arises, it's often in the form of a mid-life crisis, a divorce, loss of a career, a financial reversal, or an issue with our health. Naturally, we perceive such events negatively. But in reality this is an awakening, an amazing realization that we can choose to live a more meaningful life.

This awakening, and the journey of self-discovery it leads to, isn't a luxury but a necessity. Neither is self-exploration selfish, for awakening to who we really are isn't only a gift to ourselves but also a gift to others. Indeed, it's a step toward giving more of ourselves in the service of others. Realizing who we are and what we have to offer allows us to be truly present in our relationships, our work, and every aspect of life. The more we know and love ourselves, the more love we have available to offer others.

Parenting is our highest calling and our most important

work, so it's of tremendous value when we take responsibility for who we are and what we do. Our choices then become beneficial not only for us, but also for the people around us. Although we tend to think that life revolves around such things as money, power, status, and the stuff we amass for ourselves, the heart of life is relationships. Real happiness and a full life come from knowing ourselves, respecting ourselves, and sharing ourselves with others.

Early in my career as a teacher and therapist, I had it half right. I was sharing myself with others, listening to others, focusing on other people's issues. The problem was that I was unwilling to look at myself. Believing I was someone who was supposed to "have it together," I kept up a façade, pretending to be happy when I was actually unhappy.

It was only when the demands of parenthood invaded my life that I realized being everything to everyone was far too tiring. To be a healthy mom, wife, and human being in my own right, I needed to take care of *me*. This meant accepting my weaknesses and correcting my misperceptions. I had to let go of my need to be right, and I had to ask others for help. As I realized my worth, I increasingly made myself a priority.

To no longer imagine I needed to be perfect, and to stop pretending to be someone I wasn't, was incredibly freeing. I stopped volunteering for things I didn't want to do or taking on tasks that didn't interest me—all the things I thought I "should" do. I also enjoyed the freedom to say, "I don't know," instead of offering an uninformed response. And how freeing it was to no longer have to pretend to be happy all the time, when in reality I experienced the full range of emotions like everybody else.

It's now apparent to me when I'm acting scared, small, or guilty. I notice when I'm playing a role or pleasing someone else because I want to be accepted. And if I happen not to notice, I have loved ones who remind me to take a second look.

There's a voice in my head that likes to tell me I'm not good enough, not doing enough, and need to do more. "Keep working, keep making others happy, keep producing, keep pretending, keep tiring yourself out for the sake of others," the voices urges. But as a result of sitting in silence quite a lot so that I can hear what's going on inside me—an often uncomfortable experience—I've learned to simply observe this conversation in my head and not buy into it. Instead, I tune into my center, where there is gentleness in the deep stillness, and where I can find an ability to trust that I am indeed "enough."

I am enough even if I don't enjoy playing Barbies or dolls on the floor. I am enough when my kitchen is dirty. I am enough when I don't have an answer to your question. I am enough when my children have a tantrum in public. I am enough when I forget an appointment or have to disappoint someone.

I am enough, and so are you.

We each have our own strengths and weaknesses. We have our own unique history, along with our particular everyday circumstances. Yet in our nature we are similar, because we want the same things—to feel comfortable in our skin, to experience love, to believe in what we are doing, and to feel necessary in this world. These things can't come from external validation, which is always subjective and fleeting. To be of any value to us, they have to arise from within—from that deep "knowing" with which we were born.

Helping children retain this deep knowing is a parenting priority. Allowing our children to tell us who they are, rather than us telling them who they ought to be, is a constant necessity. It's not always easy, but it's essential if we really want them to embrace their own unique being and live the life they came here to live.

The best way to teach this is to model what it looks like. The challenge is to fully realize the life we came here to live, and to understand and appreciate who we are so that our children can see self-awareness in action. This may mean trying new things with an open mind, as well as bravely and trustingly letting go of something in our life that isn't working.

As you realize what you have to offer, you'll quite naturally come to see what your children have to offer. In the process, you'll be able to let go of the need to critique and teach all the time. Instead, you'll allow your children to inspire *you*.

Like them, you'll be free to embrace your emotions, trust your instincts, and be curious just for the sake of being curious. They'll remind you what it feels like to view the world with an open heart and mind, and to know for certain that anything is possible.

14

Touching shoulders

I GOT OFF THE TRAIN IN Chicago and headed to the corner of Madison and Canal. Though it was swamped with people, I found a place to stand as I waited for my husband to pick me up.

Noticing a tall, unkempt man walking toward me, I knew instantly he was going to ask me for money. As a Chicagoan, I'm used to being asked for money; it's part of big-city living. I usually give a dollar, some change, maybe some leftover food, or a bottle of water.

On this occasion, for some reason I experienced discomfort as he approached. In fact, I felt annoyed, asking myself, "Out of this huge crowd, why is he choosing me?"

By the time he started his sales pitch, my hand was already in my purse searching for a few dollars. As he reached for the money, he looked me in the eye and said in a quiet tone, "You know I don't want to ask for anything; you know I don't like doing this."

I held his gaze and realized his vulnerability. He almost sounded like a child. His nose was running and he looked so cold. He reminded me of my children when they need my help.

He reminded me of myself when I'm scared.

Yes, he needed money, but he was also asking for something more—validation, understanding, and compassion for his situation. Perhaps he had made some poor choices along the way, or maybe he was simply a victim of circumstances. Regardless, he just wanted to be seen. He wanted to be recognized and looked in the eye.

I placed my hand on his and said, "I know you don't want to do this. I know that."

"I want to pay this back," he said. "But if I don't see you again, I will give to somebody in your honor."

"That would be great," I replied. "Please do that."

"God bless you," he said, and I said it back. As he walked away, I drew a deep breath.

The thoughts began to flow. My professional mission is to help parents see themselves so that they can see their children. The point is for parents to grasp the importance of raising children who have a deep self-understanding and a strong sense of their worth. I try to remind them that all children belong and have a place in this world.

But does it stop there? Children grow into adults, yet this kind of reassurance is still necessary. People need to know they matter—that they belong, and that they are understood. They need to know they are not alone and that someone is willing to listen. It's important to validate our families in this way, but it's also important to offer this to our community, our city, our world. This connects us. This is what being human means.

I was at a local coffee shop writing about my experience with the man who asked me for money, when an elderly gentleman sitting nearby tried to engage me in conversation. My first response was agitation. *This is work time,* I told myself. *I must complete this article!*

Do you see the irony?

Although I was writing about my experience, I hadn't integrated the lesson. I was sharing so that I could teach, instead of practicing what I preach.

I pushed my computer aside and began to really listen and respond to this man. Initially we talked about basketball and the Final Four. But the conversation quickly turned to his life. He was eighty-five—or as he put it, "Fifty-eight, but backwards." His wife had passed away five years earlier. "She was beautiful," he reminisced, "and I miss her." He told me she loved poetry and said he liked to hand out poems she enjoyed to "spread the love." Whereupon he reached into his bag and handed me a wrinkled piece of paper with a photocopied poem, explaining that it was a special one just for me:

> *I am glad that I live, that I battle and strive*
> *For the place that I know I must fill;*
> *I am thankful for sorrows; I'll meet with a grin*
> *What fortune may send, good or ill*
> *I may not have wealth, I may not be great,*
> *But I know I shall always be true,*
> *For I have in my life that courage you gave*
> *When once I touched shoulders with you.*
> *~ Unknown*

What do we really want for our children?

WHEN I ASK PARENTS what they really want for their children, the most common response is, "I just want my kids to be happy." This is great as a concept. But as a parent, what does it mean when you say you want your children to be happy?

Do you mean that you want them to work super hard so that they are the smartest in class? Do you want them to constantly practice their sport so that they are the best athletes? Do you want them to have high grades and great test scores so that they can go to the best university? Do you want them to grow up to be rich, powerful, and famous?

I think a large slice of our culture confuses happiness with overachieving, competition, and being the "best." To want our children to be "happy" in this sense has become the norm. I suggest we've lost sight of what kids really need to live full and meaningful lives.

Above all, kids just need to be kids. They need time and space to play, dream, and be creative. I'm not just talking about in an art class, where teachers are telling them what to do. I mean open-ended time and space. A chance to be messy, dirty, and crazy creative.

INSPIRATION

Cathy Cassani Adams, LCSW, CPC, CYT

Children need downtime so that they can dive into their imagination—especially since the best imaginative play is often preceded by boredom. They need to be silly, loud, and expansive. They also need time away from television and structured activities, so that they learn to tap into their own vision, thoughts, and dreams.

Yes, children need to learn how to read, write, and do math—expressions of intelligence that come with time and practice. Their learning curve may not be in exact alignment with the school's schedule, and their pace may be different from that of their older sister or the kid they sit next to. But with educational and parental support, they'll get it.

Of far greater importance is the need for our children to develop emotional intelligence. They need to know how to be around people, the importance of taking responsibility, the art of negotiating, how to handle challenging situations, and the value of giving back to a community.

As my girls get older, I couldn't care less whether they are the smartest in their class. I just want them to be comfortable in the classroom and appreciate learning. I want them to value knowledge and stay curious. I want them to discover tools to deal with challenging academic and social experiences. I want them to enjoy great friendships, and to work well with partners and groups so that they learn how to function as a team. I want them to trust their instincts and understand that there are many definitions of the word "smart."

After watching *Race to Nowhere* one evening, I found myself emotional, almost to the point of being in pain over what's reflected in this documentary. It made me freshly aware that my hopes and dreams for my children's education are at risk in a system focused on test scores and overachieving. The movie showed wonderful teachers leaving the profession because they were expected to teach to a test, and it shared stories of children whose stress levels were so high that they wanted to leave school altogether. The pressure on kids is one of the reasons many harm themselves physically with drugs or sleep deprivation—or, worse, take their own life. Why do they want to do this? Because of a test, a class, a grade, or a non-acceptance letter from a premier university.

I loved college, and I highly recommend the experience—but not so much that I would let my children stay up all night to study, take pills to stay focused, and sacrifice their enjoyment of being themselves so that they can match up to someone else's definition of success. That's not *my* definition of success.

I expect my children to show up at school, do their best, and ask for help when they need it. I also expect them to play, have a hobby or two, go to the park, and eat dinner with the family. I want their lives to be about so much more than a test score or a grade. How they perform academically is just one aspect of their larger self, and I guarantee that class rank won't dictate their future happiness.

Some of my favorite people in the world weren't the best students. Though their grades were only fair, their lives were nevertheless full. They were social, musical, creative, and funny. Some went to college, some didn't go right away, and some didn't go at all. But almost all of them eventually found meaningful relationships and a fulfilling profession. They are still great people to be around, still full of life just like when they were young.

My grades were pretty good, but I was an awful test-taker. When I took the PSAT, my high school guidance counselor told me my score was unacceptable and that I would be unable to handle college coursework. Based on that one test, which meas-ured only a moment in time, he had the gall to determine my educational future! This individual's opinion could have dictated my life's path had I not had parents who begged to differ.

I'm in my 40s and I'm still a poor test-taker. For one thing, I see too much gray in issues, so it's hard for me to find one right answer. Yet I've pursued numerous degrees and certifica-tions, and I can't remember a time when I haven't been in school. I'm in love with learning.

I know people who were exceptional test-takers and went to the best universities. They found high-paying and high-status jobs. Yet many of them are doing work they dislike. They feel trapped by their obligations, the money, and the thought of the amount of time and effort they put into getting where they are now. Such individuals feel disconnected from their families and disconnected from themselves. They talk to me about finding their passion and about getting back to what makes them feel good. Each is living proof that perfect grades, the right university, and a high-paying job aren't guarantees of a happy life.

As parents, it's essential we are aware of the ways in which we tend to define our children based on their achievements rather than who they are. We have to catch ourselves when prais-ing them, lest we praise them for performing rather than for being good people. Is our affection and pride only reserved for academic and extracurricular achievement? Or do we see the value in our children's hobbies, relationships, and ability to know and value themselves?

I realize it's difficult to do this when family, friends, neigh-bors, and institutions say differently. It's challenging to see what's important when we are bombarded with images telling us that fame, money, and power are the most worthy achievements.

This is why we need to become acutely conscious of what we really want for our children.

We need our children to understand the importance of self-respect, compassion, and creativity. We need to teach them that while educational pursuits are valuable and necessary in our culture, formal education isn't enough. Happiness isn't about a score, a grade, an award, or a job. It's about connection to self, connection to others, and connection to this amazing planet we share together.

16

My dad, the tree of optimism

LAST WEEK MY SISTER CALLED and told me dad was being rushed to the hospital. Uncomfortable and scary for sure, but not shocking. We'd been here before.

When we arrived and the nurse asked about his medical history, my mom, sister, and I looked at each other, laughed, and said, "Where should we begin?" My dad had a minor heart attack when I was in high school, then many years later a major one that resulted in quadruple bypass surgery. While on the operating table, he had a stroke, which led to months in the ICU, followed by many more months of rehabilitation.

Although most of his functioning is back, he still struggles with aphasia, a language disorder that keeps him from recalling words. Mentally he's all there, although he can no longer effectively communicate, which is extremely frustrating for a man who spent his life teaching and telling stories.

That's not the end of it. He has diabetes, along with neuropathy in his feet. He also had skin cancer. Plus, he's undergone numerous surgeries, from having a fibrillator connected to his heart to having his gallbladder removed. This isn't the entire list, but it gives you an idea.

The crazy thing is, my dad has never been a sick person. He has never claimed to be sick, and he rarely speaks of his medical history. My sister and I joke and call it denial, but he continues to demonstrate how state of mind affects overall wellness.

During his heart surgery, we were told he wouldn't make it. A nurse actually came out and asked if we wanted to call a priest. Yet here he is still, fifteen years later. And he looks good. Sporting a better wardrobe than mine, every day—groomed and smelling good—he dresses in vibrant colors. Even with all of his physical issues, he looks younger than your average 75-year-old. He didn't even get his first gray hair until ten years ago.

It's not just about how he looks, but how he thinks. He's the king of heightened optimism, and he sees himself as lucky. He calls it Cassani luck, and he "uses" it whenever he needs it. He locates the best parking places, finds the best restaurants, and gets the best deals. While I was visiting him in the hospital last week, he told me he was in the absolute best hospital with the absolute best caretakers. Regardless of anyone else's opinion, he believes this.

My dad sees the good in everything. He smiles at people and says thank you, works hard to have conversations with people even when he can't find the words, and always hugs those he cares about. His medical chart doesn't match the way he is in life. I know he struggles. It can't be easy to have all those aches, pains, medical issues, and verbal challenges. Yet it seems he makes a decision every day to be here in the best way he can and appreciate every aspect of it.

Last week, he was admitted to the hospital because his blood sugar dropped and he was no longer coherent. When I asked him if he remembered the ambulance arriving, he said it was like a dream. He said he knew people were there, but he thought they were there because of a tree. He lives in the woods in Galena, so he's surrounded by trees. "I thought they were there to save the big tree," he explained. Well, he was right on. They were there to save the big tree of the family, the only guy surrounded by all of us girls, the optimistic center, the pillar of strength and determination to live life fully.

Just one day after being released from his two-day stay in the hospital, he decided he felt well enough to drive out with my mom and meet us for lunch. He showed up showered, shaved, and dressed in a bright orange shirt. He had big purple bruises from the multiple blood draws and hospital IV, moved slowly, and couldn't seem to find his much-needed glasses. Yet when I asked how he was doing, he replied, "Really great, hon."

I know he believes this.

He just knows it.

17

Be an amazing woman

I WATCHED OPRAH INTERVIEW Gloria Steinem. As they discussed the 2008 presidential election, Oprah mentioned the backlash she received from women when she chose to back President Obama instead of Hillary Clinton. Then she thanked Gloria, an avid Clinton supporter, for writing her a personal note during the campaign saying she fully supported Oprah's decision to choose her own candidate.

That's what it's all about—women supporting women as they make their own choices.

Choices they can make today thanks to people like Gloria Steinem, one of the countless individuals who fought for equal rights—a gift we too easily forget in this day and age.

Women have the opportunity to enhance this gift by empowering each other. But sadly, too often we choose to tear each other down. Instead of depending on each other for support and inspiration, we feel a need to compete. So if a woman has a strong opinion or disagrees with our beliefs, we're easily offended and feel we have to prove how mistaken she is. Even worse, we use words to describe her that have nothing to do with the issue at hand—slanderous words about her body, clothes, or sexual tendencies. It feels like an extension of middle school, a phase that for many of us was never resolved. Such a deeply embedded mentality desperately needs healing.

All women, young and old, need other women's support. We need to bond, hear each other, and care for each other. For when we don't care for each other, we not only inadvertently hurt ourselves, but we present a false image of womanhood to our children. They watch us as we criticize other women, especially the ones closest to us, such as our family, friends, and neighbors. Too often this criticism surrounds parenting choices—the latest issues involving birth, nursing, co-sleeping, discipline, or whether it's better to work or stay at home.

Instead of hearing and respecting each other, we fight about who's right. We argue over who's the better mother, as if it was an argument we could actually win. Our children watch reality shows in which women hit each other, yell at each other, give their bodies away, and compete for a man or a better house. They listen to music in which women are called bitches or whores, and they sing along as if it's normal.

Instead of accepting so many untruths about women and passing along so much misinformation, we need to *claim* ourselves so that our children can *see* us. Our daughters, yes. But just as importantly our sons, because our boys need to understand and honor womanhood.

Strong, aware women innately know how to listen and empathize. They understand how to validate and support. Hence they have the kind of gifts that build trust, lessen the fear of vulnerability, and make it easier to share ideas and find common ground. So why do we so often look to others for direction and validation instead of trusting who we came here to be? Why do we forget to love ourselves, neglecting our strengths?

To disrupt this negative cycle, we need to know without a shadow of doubt that we are important and worthy. One of the ways we can help each other in this is by adopting a philosophy of *no comparison, no competition.*

I don't want to spend my time comparing my skills or my body to those of another. There's no reason for me to try to be superior or to feel inferior in the presence of other women. When I experience feelings of frustration, envy, or other ego-based emotions, I acknowledge that they aren't being caused by someone else. They are the result of my intolerance, my judgment, my limited thinking. They are my misconceptions, my fears, my issues to work on, and it's unfair to blame other women as if they were my enemy.

I admit it's not always easy. There are times when I need to work through my annoyance and perhaps have a good cry. But for the most part, the *no comparison, no competition* mentality offers me peace, a freedom that's hard to describe.

As a result, many new and amazing women have come into my life. Women I learn from and women I get to teach. Women who allow me to support them, and women who support me when I'm in need. We get to hold each other up and honor both our similarities and differences. By depending on each other in this way, we naturally become better partners, business people, leaders, and mothers.

We also no longer need to look like a photo-shopped image in a magazine, make as much money as our neighbor, shame ourselves for our past, tell ourselves we aren't good enough, be angry with people who don't look or think like we do, or disparage women behind their backs. Free of such burdens, we realize we have a lot more energy at our disposal, which allows us to take care of ourselves instead of being exhausted all the time.

As we at last appreciate, maybe for the first time, the joy of being a woman, we gain a deeper appreciation for the women who surround us. Our contentment increases, our trust grows, our communication improves, and our children get to watch us love and take care of each other. They learn from an early age how amazing it is to be a woman, as well as how beautiful it is to be loved by a woman.

Help your kids practice bravery

I WATCH MY THREE DAUGHTERS do new things every day. They walk into a new classroom, talk to a new kid at the park, begin a new sport or activity, ride a bigger bike. Most of us have watched them venture out like this, but I wonder whether we recognize our bravery as well as our children's bravery.

Every day children put themselves out there, try new things, walk through new doors. We expect them to do these things, and we may chastise them if they don't. When a child cries or admits discomfort, we perhaps even use guilt or shame to quiet them rather than acknowledge their feelings.

Life involves risk. It calls for a willingness to be vulnerable. We can't be brave if we don't realize there's something to lose. Admitting fear or expressing concern is brave in itself. Asking someone to support us or sharing our deepest thoughts takes a great deal of courage.

As adults, we can easily fall into a routine or get into our groups and stop trying new things, stop putting ourselves out there. We find a no-risk zone so that we don't have to deal with failure or being criticized. Yet when our kids hesitate to step into a new experience, we are either annoyed or confused by

INSPIRATION
Cathy Cassani Adams, LCSW, CPC, CYT

their tears and worries. We find ourselves telling them how to feel, and why they are wrong, rather than listening to their honest and heartfelt concerns.

Since children are expected to take risks all the time, can we see their experiences through their eyes? When they say they are scared, they are looking for validation and normalizing. They are asking for help, hoping the ones they love most will understand and guide them through their fears. The goal is not to talk them out of their fear, but to acknowledge and allow for it. In this way, we support them as they navigate their new experience.

Might we also share with them that sometimes we feel afraid? That when we try new things, it's not easy for us either? Our ability to acknowledge and listen offers a sense of normalcy and fuels their determination to keep going. It gives them the foundation they need to practice bravery.

INTROSPECTION

*When you think everything is someone else's fault, you will suffer a lot.
When you realize everything springs only from yourself,
you will learn both peace and joy.*

DALAI LAMA

19

Pretending kind of sucks

SOMETIMES I'M AN EXTROVERT. I love being with people, whether it's talking to groups, teaching classes, or laughing with my friends and family. My life is full because of these experiences and relationships.

At other times I'm an introvert. I have days when I need space and quiet and crave being alone. I don't always understand why, but I try to accept such times and trust there are reasons.

This wasn't always the case. I used to hide the introverted part of myself, since I received more kudos for my extroverted nature and wasn't always comfortable with comments such as, "What's wrong? Are you okay? You don't seem like yourself." Because being quiet and contemplative seemed to cause concern, I worked hard to be social and talkative.

Basically, I would just pretend.

My inability to accept myself as someone who needs downtime—someone who doesn't always love small talk, but who requires space—caused me not only to pretend, but to secretly blame others for *forcing* me to pretend.

Consequently, instead of owning that sometimes I needed space and time alone, I'd get annoyed with people who unknowingly infringed on my need for quiet. It might be the person who knocked on my door, the neighbor who wanted to chat, or the friend who called on the phone. *How dare they bother me!* I'd tell myself. *Don't they know that right now I don't have the energy to pretend?*

But really, how could they know? After all, it was I who taught them I'm available 24/7. Not only available, but constantly talkative and upbeat. I showed them I have all the time and energy in the world for them.

The beauty of age and the increasing self-awareness that can come with it is that I finally realized the silliness of this. It dawned on me that it was *my* responsibility to offer myself authentically, which meant teaching people how to treat me. I need to let them know that sometimes I want to talk with people, and sometimes I want to be by myself. Sometimes I want to carpool, and sometimes I want to drive alone. Sometimes I want to go to a movie with friends, and sometimes I want to be in a theater all by myself.

After some practice, I find I can do this without making up excuses, lying, or feeling there's something wrong with me.

And honestly, pretending is just tiring and kind of sucks. I find it takes a toll on my energy, spirit, and overall well-being. Pretending to care when I don't, or that I don't when I do. Pretending to be someone I'm not. Pretending everything's okay when it isn't. How exhausting it all is!

I try to keep in mind how detrimental pretense is when I parent my girls. I don't want them to pretend around me. Like me, they have different sides, and they need space to be who they are. If they are quiet, it doesn't always mean it's something I need to worry about. If they are grumpy, it doesn't mean they are ungrateful or disrespectful. To tell them they shouldn't be angry, quiet, introspective, or sad is a disservice.

To expect them to always be playful or smiling isn't realistic. Of course, if my kids are "happy" all the time, I get to feel good. I also get to be the great parent with the constantly happy kids. Until I realize I'm caught in the cycle of pretending all over again.

So really, it's an exercise in tolerance. Can I tolerate the fact that I may disappoint someone when I tell them I need to be alone? Can I tolerate the fact that they may not be very accepting of me? Can I be okay if my kids are feeling quiet, frustrated, or unsocial?

It benefits all of us to recognize that authenticity, which requires us to embrace the natural ebb and flow of life, is a normal part of being a human being. For me, this requires taking yet another step toward self-acceptance.

Some days, I must sit in the discomfort of not being who people think I should be and know in my heart this is a good thing. Because in such moments, I'm fully embracing who I am.

INTROSPECTION
Cathy Cassani Adams, LCSW, CPC, CYT

20

Why a man needs to ask a woman if she's okay—and why he needs to ask again

As WOMEN, WE CAN LAUGH about needing to be asked ten times if we are "okay." We identify with it, normalize it, and validate other women when they have the same need. But the best thing we can do is learn from it.

When a man asks if you are okay, he wants to know if you are okay. He's noticed you're somehow different. Perhaps you seem annoyed, put out, distant. So he asks how you are.

Of course, you tell him you're "fine." So he takes you at your word. That's because men don't really beat around the bush with one another, but say what they are thinking. He expects you to do the same.

Instead, you get mad. You think he should do more, maybe ask a different way. In fact, now that you think about it, if he really cared, he should just "know." This seems rational to you, but it's irrational to him.

I know this because I used to do it all the time. My husband would ask whether I was okay, and I'd tell him I was fine. Except that I wasn't. Then I'd get mad when he didn't ask again, telling him he didn't care, or even that he didn't love me enough.

The truth is, *I* didn't love me enough. I was the one who didn't speak the truth, who acted passive-aggressively instead of being honest. I was the one who created my suffering, which was a double-edged sword in that I'd suffer when I didn't say what I really wanted to say, and suffer when I didn't feel understood. I can't guarantee someone will understand and empathize with me, but I certainly can't expect them to until I speak honestly.

Like me, many women my age have difficulty saying what they mean because we were taught to please others. We were taught that expressing frustration is unbecoming, irrational, dramatic, and unkind. Through both words and actions, we learned we might not be liked if we showed anger, sadness, or in fact any negative emotion.

As females, we were taught that we were to be nice, good, agreeable, and to put others first. We learned to push our true feelings aside and suck it up for the sake of everyone else. Which is why it was difficult for me to say what I was really feeling. Instead, I'd get angry, then immediately feel terrified the person would reject me for being angry.

In my mind, I'd ask myself, "Will he think I'm disagreeable? Will he think I'm high maintenance? Will he think I'm annoying, dramatic—or, God forbid, unlovable?"

I had to take a risk and break the passive-aggressive habit. Tired of suffering in silence, I had to share what I was feeling.

At first I told my husband to just keep asking me until I was able to tell him the truth. Although this didn't really make sense to him, he obliged. Pretty quickly, he only needed to ask five times, then three, then once.

Finally, he didn't need to ask me at all. I went to *him* when

I was disappointed, confused, or hurt. Instead of wallowing in my emotions and waiting for him to notice, I told him I needed to share how I was feeling and asked him to simply listen. And that was the end of it.

In other words, instead of blaming my husband for everything and criticizing him for not "getting me," I helped him understand. He did his part too, exercising the patience and understanding to really listen and hear me. Because we're different, this wasn't always easy for him, since what I feel and experience doesn't necessarily make sense to him—and vice versa. But that's the point of partnership or friendship, to grow and learn from each other. To slow down, listen, and empathize, even when it doesn't completely make sense.

My husband could have just stayed stuck, telling himself, "I don't get women." Or he could be patient and really get to know a woman. By setting aside his defenses and his need to be right, he would realize I was looking for the same thing he was looking for—love and understanding. Understanding doesn't mean complete agreement, and neither does it mean allowing me to "win." He doesn't have to give in or agree with everything I say. He just needs to hear me, see me, trust me, and accept me as I am. But this can only happen if I speak up, being honest about how I feel even if it causes me to feel vulnerable. Indeed, I need to state my insecurities and fears. This is what love and intimacy are all about.

It's for this reason that a spouse, friend, or even a child can be a great spiritual teacher. We love them enough to be willing to look at ourselves and take ownership of our actions and issues. They inspire us to go beyond our comfortable habits and take responsibility for what we bring to the relationship.

Have I mastered speaking my mind and sharing my

vulnerabilities? No. But I practice every day. Since I like to feel comfortable, sometimes I fall back into old habits. But eventually I notice, and then I do my best to get real and start over.

Girls are mean?

"GIRLS ARE MEAN." It's a comment that makes me cringe because it's not a fair statement. If you are like me, you know many fantastic girls and women. Smart, funny, intelligent, strong, loving, kind, giving, powerful girls and women. Have they ever been mean? Probably. Haven't we all? The fact that a girl *can* be mean doesn't mean girls are generically mean. Meanness is a human issue, not a female issue.

However, the more we say girls are mean, the more these words take on a life of their own, creating a collective belief. Making statements of this kind then tends to influence how girls feel about themselves and how they are treated. It pits girls against each other, creating a distrust, a need to compete, and a desire to emotionally and physically harm—something we see all too much of on reality television.

I have three young girls, and professionally I've worked with many young girls, so I've witnessed meanness more than once. Of course young girls have mean moments—I had them myself. But let's talk about meanness as *behavior,* rather than as an overriding character trait.

Quite the contrary to girls being mean, one of the outstanding things about females is their sensitivity, which is an especially female gift. Not that men don't have it, but in females it's heightened. However, in our society, sensitivity is seen as weakness. So when girls feel sadness, pain, and anger, their sensitivity is referred to as "drama." Consequently it can be a struggle for girls, as well as women, to share intense feelings. Society expects females to be "kind" and "polite" all the time.

When girls demonstrate mean behavior, often it's because they've been taught to be selfless, which means they have to limit their self-expression. They aren't allowed to express what they are feeling or what they need. But when females have difficulty speaking their mind and sharing their feelings without being shamed or ridiculed, it can lead to them swallowing their emotions. Inevitably this swallowed pain comes out as passive-aggressive behavior, such as talking behind people's backs, which is a form of meanness. Even more damaging, it can result in self-loathing, guilt, and depression.

Bullying is an extreme example of meanness, but it originates in suppressed emotion. Bullies bully because they feel hurt and because they are insecure. Their behavior is an attempt to cover up the fact that they feel powerless, to the point of being uncomfortable in their own skin. Inflicting pain on others is a way of spreading their pain around in the hope of releasing it. Although such behavior should never be tolerated, it's important to understand what's driving it.

Young girls need the space and understanding to be able to share their feelings, say what they mean, disagree, be bold, be authentically themselves, and be accepted. Their sensitivity and intuitiveness needs to be recognized and celebrated rather than ridiculed.

If you tell your daughter that girls are mean, you're telling her she is, too. This is a huge disservice to her understanding of what it means to be female.

Females are truth tellers who feel the truth in their bodies. They also feel other people's pain and experience anger when people are mistreated. They feel love intensely, laugh loudly, and enjoy sharing their joy. Not only do they give birth to children, but they are gifted with creativity. They are leaders, athletes, caregivers, influencers, mothers, nurturers, and protectors.

What we believe is what we tend to see, and what we imagine often becomes our reality. For this reason, it's important to honor who we are as females and choose carefully what we say to each other. Then our daughters will grow up as gifted, sensitive individuals with unlimited potential.

22

Gray hair

THE DAY FINALLY ARRIVED when I became aware of a lot of gray hairs. During the course of the last year, I've found a few; but now I'm seeing a lot. As I mentioned, my dad didn't get gray hair until his sixties; and my sister is two years older than I and just found her first. No doubt I'm genetically lucky when it comes to the gray hair department, so for me it isn't an issue of vanity or a rant about aging.

It's just that when I stare at my hair, it seems crazy that I can actually have gray hair and still act like a twelve-year-old. I don't mean conceptually, but *truly* act like my old twelve-year-old self. This is because, when I have to deal with any form of confrontation, my inner twelve-year-old starts to worry and becomes scared.

The little girl of twelve wants to make sure everyone is comfortable, and that she isn't making herself seem too important. She does this because she's a typical middle school girl who desperately wants to be accepted and liked.

Sometimes, when my husband and I are arguing, my twenty-two-year-old self comes out. She wants him to know she's tough. Not just tough, but right. She also wants to make sure he knows she's independent and wise—although the truth is, she's afraid of not being loved. She desperately wants to be seen and acknowledged by someone she cares about.

The worst is when I'm frustrated with my children, because then my inner seven-year-old makes an appearance. One of my daughters says something disrespectful, and out comes a childish comeback. Anything said with childlike bravado tends not to come out sounding very mature, let alone kind.

The woman in the mirror is a grown-up, but all of her different behaviors at various ages still live inside her. They still clamor to be heard, and they want to offer protection from pain. These aspects of myself at different ages come out when I feel uncomfortable, afraid, or when I'm unaware. In other words, they make an appearance when I'm living on autopilot. Although they shouldn't be stepping into a present-day issue, they do so because they want to protect, defend, guard. For this, I understand and honor them. I see what they are trying to do. I understand they are attempting to use techniques that worked long ago.

Except that it's no longer the past and things are different.

When we read present-day experiences through an old filter, they skew our perspective. Because they are loaded with old hurt and outdated beliefs, they create misunderstandings and spawn vicious cycles. Showing up in the present like this, they do more harm than good.

As adults, we are responsible to integrate and honor these aspects of ourselves, while ensuring they don't take over our present. If we unconsciously continue to view our life through the eyes of a seven, twelve, or twenty-two-year-old, we are bound to have some issues!

Behavior associated with certain ages, replete with the defenses we used at that age, will inevitably pop up at different times. The challenge is to notice when this is happening. Then we can let the younger version of ourselves know that the person we are today can handle whatever's happening.

This is an exercise in being here, now. It's what it means to be in the moment, to let the past go, to be free. Though we need to acknowledge our past hurts and experiences, we don't need to drag them around with us everywhere we go. At the time, they offered us an opportunity to grow. But if we stay stuck in them, we can't evolve.

At seven, I needed to know how to talk back in an argument. At twelve, I needed to conform and keep the peace. At twenty-two, I needed to appear strong and not let others know they hurt me. Each of these was my truth back then. But they aren't my truth today. The needs I had back then are outdated and unnecessary.

So my gray hair turns out to be another reminder to be where I am—forty-three, and increasingly conscious. I appreciate the years of experience that brought me to this day, this moment, and this hair color.

Needing approval: the childhood wound that keeps showing up

WHEN WE WERE LITTLE, approval was essential for our survival. In our birth family, we had to do and say what others deemed appropriate. We needed approval so that our basic needs would be met. Later, socially we sought approval to create friendships. Peers made us feel part of something, connecting us to something bigger than ourselves. These are the most impactful and fundamental contributors to our journey toward acceptance, the initial relationships that allow us to survive and thrive in society.

As we grow older, other people's approval is no longer essential for our survival. Of course, we want to maintain our family connections, along with our important friendships, and we appreciate recognition from others. But as adults, we can meet our basic needs. Other people's approval is a bonus rather than essential.

When someone doesn't accept us, it may initially resurrect a deep fear from childhood—the sense that it's unsafe not to comply with other people's expectations. However, such fear is really quite ungrounded in most cases, since the truth is that in most families our needs would have been met even if we didn't earn approval. Of course, young children with growing brains don't tend to know this, since they think in black and white and either feel loved, which is a safe feeling, or not loved, which is an unsafe feeling.

When such ideas are carried into adulthood, they show up in ways that affect our adult choices.

The fear of not being loved—of not gaining the approval we crave—is perhaps our most common fear as human beings. If someone is unkind to us in person, says something nasty on social networking, breaks up with us, chooses another instead of us, flips us off in traffic, or doesn't hire us for a job, it can take us back to that childhood fear of feeling unloved, unaccepted, unsafe.

Our challenge is to recognize that this is no longer true, and in fact may never have been true. The fear of finding ourselves disconnected from others is an old wound, or an old misunderstanding. Our fear that some may not approve of us today is a mere echo of that wound or misunderstanding. Unless we buy into it, it in no way threatens our ability to survive and thrive in the present. Yes, it might be uncomfortable, and it may even hurt. But that initial fear we feel that causes us to reel, brings us to our knees, or provokes us to go on the attack, is likely not our present day situation, but simply the old wound.

When someone doesn't approve, or says something unkind, it's possible to respond in a way that's consistent with the reality of this moment. Maybe the first step is to listen for anything we can learn, since there's often a piece of truth in the most misguided of statements. If the person is irrational or intends us harm, we need to realize it's their own pain they are dealing with and has nothing to do with us.

If we want to take it deeper, we can allow the situation to

remind us to be more accepting of others instead of disparaging or judgmental. Feeling either the sting of the present day accusation or the old wound can become a powerful reminder to be more caring toward and accepting of others.

The more we can accept others, the faster our fear of being unaccepted fades. Not because we've become tough and uncaring, but because we are becoming compassionate and empathic. In so doing, we regain our foundation, which grounds us in living in the moment. We recognize we're safe, right now, right here.

As for other people, if they can't accept us, it's their issue, not something we need to fix or even concern ourselves with. To be able to handle other people's negative opinions or decisions without internalizing them or retaliating is an empowered state. It's what real strength entails.

Equally, to be able to accept ourselves without needing the approval of others is a barometer of maturity.

24

The grass is green on both sides

ONCE IN A WHILE, I get to be alone. Not just for a little while, but for a full day and night. This is quite uncommon; but when it happens, it's a welcome experience. Although I love my extroverted high-intensity time with my family and friends, as I've mentioned, part of me is quite introverted. I love being alone.

I didn't fully believe this until my first baby came and it was never quiet. I experienced anxiety and the feeling that I needed to escape, if only for a little while, to the grocery store or to fill my car's gas tank. You know you need to be alone when these activities become "fun."

Then the second baby came, and the third. Soon it seemed someone was always talking to me, asking me for things, to the point that I felt I was living in a state of constant disruption. My days consisted of half-sentences, half-thoughts, and I racked up innumerable unmade points and forgotten ideas. Not easy for a chronically introspective person like myself, who revels in processing the most mundane things thoroughly.

As the mom in the family, it isn't always possible for me to be my typically reflective self, since my reality requires me to be "on" for four other people. To keep my sanity, I needed to find tools that could offer me a release. For example, I take notes whenever I have a deep thought. I journal, as well as blog. I talk and process on our radio show. I also give it my best effort to get in ten minutes of quiet in the mornings, though this isn't always possible.

When I do my best to respect the introverted aspect of my nature, I find that my extroverted self enjoys taking on the demands of family and the daily schedule of dropping off, picking up, helping with homework, eating together, and talking over the day—along with reading books together, watching a movie, and getting ready for bed. This daily routine provides me with structure, which fosters a feeling of stability, as well as a feeling of connectedness and meaning.

So I live in a paradox, an aspect of which is that when I'm experiencing one half of who I am, I often find myself thinking about the other half. In practice, this means that when I'm with my family at the dinner table, I have passing thoughts of eating alone while reading a magazine. But when I'm alone in a restaurant, I longingly look at the families who are eating together. I enjoy quietly reading a book on the couch, although the mere process brings to mind reading a favorite book with my kids. And when I have a rare opportunity to sleep in, I find myself longing for a wake-up call from my favorite little people.

I wouldn't want you to think I'm complaining or not appreciating my life moment-by-moment. Quite the opposite, I embrace the paradox and realize it's exactly how things are supposed to be. To be alone, and to need to be needed, are both essential for my well-being. Neither status decreases or threatens my love of the other.

Though I may think about the other when I'm experiencing one aspect of myself, I'm also aware that the grass *isn't* greener over there. My thoughts may drift, yet I'm acutely aware it's not time for over there, but time to be here.

Like right now. I'm writing in the quiet of my office. Every now and again, I forget I'm alone and turn as if to say something to my husband. A few minutes ago, I heard something that sounded like my daughter's cough. And when I hear creaking upstairs, I think it's one of the girls playing. Except that they aren't here, and I'm by myself.

During this time alone, I've completed so many tasks, sat and stared out the window, played my own music, turned myself inside out with introspection, and felt gratitude for the silence. Simultaneously, I miss all the sounds. I miss my family.

I stayed present throughout my evening alone, enjoyed a few movies, and eventually fell asleep. In the morning, I awakened to find everyone home earlier than expected because my husband was sick. The girls wanted to shower, and then they needed to go to the library. The car had to be unpacked, the laundry get done. Dinner needed to be made, as did lunches for the next morning.

I smiled as I thought about the slowness of yesterday, the time available for introspection, the rare opportunity for so many personal choices. What a different day today has been. But as I found my thoughts drifting, I became acutely aware that it wasn't time for over there.

It was time for *here.*

INTROSPECTION
Cathy Cassani Adams, LCSW, CPC, CYT

25

Need peace? Drop into your heart

WORRY DOESN'T HELP ANYTHING. Giving it our attention is a useless activity, not to mention a drain on our whole being. Staying stuck in it skews our judgment and perception. We can forever analyze the worry that lives in our endlessly processing brain, or we can let it go and move into the heart.

Since we've been trained to be brain-centric, this isn't always easy. The thinking mind likes to think, so it may feel threatened by your desire to feel with the heart. It may try to convince you that brain power far exceeds that of the heart, and therefore it needs to be in charge.

For this reason, moving into the heart requires practice, and sometimes I think I'll forever be a student. But it's worth the energy because it offers peace. Letting go of our worries and shifting into the heart, even momentarily, allows us to see that worrisome thoughts are indeed just thoughts, not reality.

Many wise teachers have explained the importance of shifting from mind to heart, but I like to use author Martha Beck's idea of *dropping into* the heart. I like it because it feels doable, involving a real shift rather than mere adherence to a concept.

When you drop into your heart, you *feel* instead of

think. Instead of being focused on past experiences or concerns about what might go wrong in the future, you are just here, now. And when you are here, everything is okay. Of course, if you go back to your thoughts, they'll tell you differently. But your heart is smarter. Your heart is *you*.

The more we practice "dropping in," perhaps using a practice such as meditation or prayer—or simply in everyday moments—the more it becomes natural, and the more that heart-centeredness spreads into other areas of our lives.

When I started this practice, I noticed my sternum was physically sore, as if something was opening up inside me. I still occasionally feel a gentle soreness, and I use it as a reminder to keep opening, keep working the wisest muscle in the body.

There are times—sometimes days, even weeks—when my mind takes over and I lose the practice. I get lost in thought and forget that my mind isn't my most efficient problem solver. As Einstein said, we can't solve a problem with the same kind of thinking we used when we created it. I even question the idea of "thinking a problem through." Not because I don't honor the brain's abilities, but because core answers don't come from thinking. They come from feeling.

If you are truly struggling, you don't need more thought. You need quiet. Then, in the stillness, you feel what to do next. In this way, problem-solving becomes an exercise in trusting yourself.

Breathing, give your brain a rest and drop into your heart. As you do so, you'll feel what I can best describe as hope. When I say hope, I'm not talking about the future, but about an experience of transcendence and grace right here, right now, in which you shift down into your heart, the real you—the part of you that's connected to the greater wisdom. In effect, you're reconnecting with the feeling of peace that was your ongoing state as a child.

Whenever you are sad, grieving, afraid, angry, or lonely, the heart's the place to go. Don't search for answers outside yourself, because they're already inside you. They've always been there. You just have to bring your attention back to the knowing part of you. As Glinda said to Dorothy, "You've always had the power to go back to Kansas."

If you're unsure about what I'm saying, try this: Point to yourself right now. What are you pointing to?

See, you know.

26

Creativity and impressing the one who matters most

"Every child is an artist," said Pablo Picasso. "The problem is to remain an artist once they grow up."

When I was little, I wanted to fly. In an attempt to remain suspended in mid-air, I'd jump from tables and chairs, using fly swatters as wings. Or I'd hold an umbrella. It was all very exciting.

Along with my enthusiasm for flying, I dove into art projects, baked cakes from scratch that were usually inedible, wrote and told stories, and would swing *really* high on the swings. I also spent a lot of time singing in front of the mirror. I was uninterested in outcomes, only in the process of creating, expanding, sharing.

At some point my enthusiasm for these simple things of life began to fade. As it did so, the way I saw myself also changed. "Creative" and "artistic" were dropped from my personal descriptors. Age, education, and comparing myself with others changed everything, as my inability to be considered the "best" at anything art-related, along with the hard focus on a "real" career path, ate away at my spirit.

INTROSPECTION
Cathy Cassani Adams, LCSW, CPC, CYT

Somewhere along the way, I stopped feeling content. Because I needed several degrees, I strove hard. But as I did so, I increasingly felt uncomfortable in my own skin.

With my own innate creativity no longer in the picture, it was as if there was a hole in my center—an emptiness that drove me to seek the approval of others. Because I couldn't hear or feel myself anymore, I fell into the habit of allowing others to tell me who to be and how to do things.

Then one day, after having my first baby, I felt so panicked, lost, and afraid that I picked up a pen and started to write. My disillusionment, fear, and inability to sense myself came out on paper. And when I was done, I was so uncomfortable, I felt like I had thrown up. Yet the process left me feeling so much better. Something that was beyond me reconnected, allowing me to feel and tell my truth again.

Writing became a release. Even more profound, it became time spent in pure spirit. I felt lighter, more fluid, and I saw good in life again. Stuff just came up and came through, and I was able to share it. Today, my work is all about creativity, all about feeling the flow.

This doesn't mean that comparison and competition aren't still alive, distracting me at times and pushing me back into the approval-hungry zone. But when everything begins to feel too heavy, I close my eyes and see the girl who flew, baked, made a mess, and swung so high. And she says to me in her kid voice, "Why do you do that?"

I like her—she's awesome. She doesn't relate to my self-imposed external demands. She only knows what feels right. And I love listening to her. She's the one I want to impress. Not with awards, status, and recognition, but with the freedom to speak, play, and be who she came here to be.

Personal truth and the need to please

I'VE BECOME ENAMORED with people who speak their truth and stay strong in the face of loud disagreement. People who honor what they know, do what's right, and move forward even when others pressure them to back down.

Lincoln, Thomas Merton, Gandhi, Martin Luther King, Jr., John Keating from Dead Poets Society, and even Merida from Brave are some of my favorite touchstones. Not because they were perfect, but because they stood by what they believed. They trusted what they knew.

Isn't this an important aspect of our purpose in life—to share what we know?

Even though some may believe they have all the answers, nobody "owns" the truth. Each of us has our own truth, our own gifts, our own messages to share. We all have an important place in the world. Every single one of us is needed in this time and space.

Sometimes sharing a personal truth causes agitation or triggers defensiveness. Some become insistent that one way is right and all others wrong. However, life isn't that cut and dried. We each have a set of different experiences to draw upon, and our understanding is affected by our particular situation, including the choices we've made and their outcome. We can't help but see the world through the eyes of our unique story.

I feel inspired to write about love. Not the romantic kind of love, but the sort that involves self-acceptance, honoring others, and a sense that we're "all in this together." As I write, I recognize there's no way to perfect this kind of love. Making mistakes and coming up against challenges are intrinsic to the love I'm referring to. It's a kind of love that's most evident when we forgive, and when we stay focused on the inherent goodness of others in the face of negativity.

My approach to love resonates with some, while others see it differently, and still others disagree loudly. The loud group view the world from a different perspective than mine; and when they share their opinion, it isn't to try to have a conversation, but out of a need to be right. We see this in politics, on the internet, and even on the playground. The game is about who can scream the loudest, who can be the most intimidating.

For me, learning to share what I believe has been a long road and is ongoing. It's been a matter of learning to stay grounded when confronted with either real-time or virtual comments, saying what feels true to me instead of quieting down because of discomfort or out of a need to please. It's been an adventure in discovering my personal truth, being open about it, and embracing Joseph Campbell's wonderful insight that "the privilege of a lifetime is being who you are."

We can love others, learn from them, and listen intently to what they have to share. But when it becomes hurtful, loud, or feels like a game of win-or-lose, we can let go of the need to please and trust in what our heart aches to say. We can channel those who have been here before us, together with the fictional characters who inspire us—those who stood strong even in the face of great adversity.

EMOTION

The fastest way to freedom is to feel your feelings.

GITA BELLIN

28

Do your children feel emotionally safe?

EVERYWHERE I TURN there are news alerts and articles about how to protect children physically. How to keep them from being hurt. How to keep them safe in school, on their bikes, in the car. Important and necessary, yes. But it makes me wonder why we don't focus as much attention on children's *emotional* safety. Why aren't we just as vigilant about their emotional well-being, their spirit, their "beingness," their "I AMness?"

I see an urgent need to direct more energy into this phase of our children's development. It's important to encourage parents to be more aware of and invested in what's going on inside their children. It's also crucial to keep in mind that everyday interactions have an impact on our children's emotional well-being.

How can we make emotional safety a priority? I have a number of suggestions:

1. Allow your children to ask questions and offer a different perspective without evaluating what they are saying. Especially don't shame them or make them feel guilty.

EMOTION
Cathy Cassani Adams, LCSW, CPC, CYT

2. Allow your children to express emotion, even when this involves uncomfortable feelings such as sadness or anger.

3. Allow your children to have their own life. Don't ask them to take on your dreams.

4. Get out of teaching mode, be quiet, and listen.

5. Touch them lovingly—hugs, hand holding, massages, or an arm around the shoulder.

6. Trust that your children know who they are, and above all don't tell them who to be.

7. Trust that your children are innately good.

8. Teach your children to believe in love, not fear.

9. When it's necessary to allow your children to fail so that they can learn life's lessons, be their greatest cheerleader and supporter as they pick up the pieces.

10. Remember that bringing up a child means teaching, understanding, respecting, communicating, and listening. It doesn't mean instilling fear.

11. Put the phone down and shut off the computer so that you can offer your undivided attention.

12. *See* your children, and let them know you see them. Offer smiles, eye contact, high fives, thumbs up, fist bumps—whatever works.

13. Make the house, or at least a space in the house, calm and peaceful, so that when quiet is needed, it can be found.

14. Allow your children to be children. Don't burden them with adult problems and issues.

LIVING WHAT YOU WANT YOUR KIDS TO LEARN
Cathy Cassani Adams, LCSW, CPC, CYT

15. No more over-scheduling your children. Let them play!

16. Don't place conditions on your love, and stop saying, "I love you, *but*…." If you say, "I love you," end it with a period.

17. Get out of the past, but don't jump into the future. Focus on today and *this* moment.

18. Love yourself, heal yourself, nurture yourself, make yourself a priority, deal with your issues, ask for help, and don't be a martyr. Like it or not, you are your children's role model for emotional safety.

Instead of focusing on *doing*, our focus needs to be on *being*. We can help our children embrace who they are so that they trust themselves. And we can help them accept *what is* so that they more easily flow with the ups and downs of life. It's simply a matter of reexamining and redefining what it means to feel truly safe, inside and out.

29

Why feeling emotion is essential for you and your kids

WOULDN'T IT BE GREAT if we could just feel the good feelings? If we could bypass what makes us feel disappointed, sad, or uncomfortable?

While it would be wonderful to just feel love, joy, and a sense of peace, emotions are a package deal. We either feel them all, or it's difficult to feel anything at all.

This doesn't mean we have to suffer when painful feelings arise. To illustrate what I mean, we can acknowledge anxiety without becoming a worrier. We can feel the injustice of something without flying into a rage. Emotions don't have to become a mode of being.

Too often we feel something, then push it away for fear of becoming angry, weak, or extremely sad. When we do so, we suppress the natural signals our body sends us to keep us aware.

Denying what we are feeling leads to a state of repression. Shoved out of sight, the emotion morphs into a *state*, such as constant anxiety, impatience, or a critical spirit. Such dysfunctional patterns of behavior become a hallmark of our personality. Consequently, we're mad at everything, but we don't know why;

or sad much of the time, without anything in particular causing us sadness in the moment.

Emotions aren't the problem. It's our inability to fully feel our emotions that gets us in trouble. If we would just allow a feeling to come up, let the tears flow, face up to whatever it's about—such as what's making us angry—the emotion wouldn't fester. Once acknowledged and felt, it can be released. Then we don't waste our valuable energy pretending not to feel a certain way when we obviously do, or telling ourselves and others that things don't bother us when everyone can see how bothered we are.

Distracting ourselves from what we are feeling—denying our emotions—is commonly referred to as numbing. This takes many forms, such as excessive use of alcohol, overeating, indulging in drugs or medicating ourselves, being a shopaholic, spending all our spare time with technology, and staying busy, which is the most socially acceptable form of numbing. How often do we keep ourselves busy so that we don't have to deal with how we're truly feeling? By being perpetually busy, we keep our focus away from what's going on inside us, preferring anything to having to feel.

The really sad part about this is that anything going on inside us isn't trying to harm us. It doesn't come into our lives to hurt us. Rather, it's trying to heal us, moving us toward greater wholeness. Its objective is to help us let go of something we no longer need in our lives, which enables us to return to a more peaceful way of being.

Children get this. They know how to have a good cry, and they know how to express disapproval or call out something that seems unjust. But what do we do when they express what they are feeling? We order them to "stop it." We tell them they are being manipulative, too dramatic, or insensitive. In this way, we teach them their emotions aren't desirable. So they learn to numb out and pretend.

What if we felt our feelings instead? What if we actually accepted our emotions, neither reacting to them nor suppressing them, but allowing them to pass through us?

To take this approach to our emotions is to appreciate our body's natural ability to release what it doesn't need. It also empowers us to teach our kids to do the same. We could share tools that would help them appropriately discuss and release whatever they may be feeling. In this way they learn to honor their feelings.

All of us—parents and children—need to embrace our emotions as normal, as an essential aspect of being human. Whether it's a good feeling or not-so-good feeling, we all need to give ourselves and each other permission to feel it fully.

30

Let your child be unhappy

ONE MORNING SKYLAR was frustrated. She wanted a waffle, she wanted her seat cleaned, and she wanted me to push her chair in. For no obvious reason, she had woken up frustrated. The more she whined, the more I too began to feel frustrated.

I mentioned that her tone wasn't kind and told her she needed to be patient. "I'm doing the best I can to make breakfast for everyone," I explained.

"It just needs to come out," she said. "It won't come out."

"What needs to come out?" I inquired.

"My sads," she said.

When I told her it was okay to let them out, everything changed. She turned to her dad, who was right next to her. Sitting on his lap, she cried and cried, while he hugged her. We didn't talk, didn't demand to know what was wrong. We simply allowed her to cry, while I continued to make breakfast for her sisters.

I have no idea what Sky was releasing. Maybe it was a bad dream or an issue from the day before or the previous week. Whatever it was, she knew it was time to let it go. Equally important, she needed the space and support to do so.

EMOTION

Cathy Cassani Adams, LCSW, CPC, CYT

All three of my daughters practice this. Not all the time, but when things really build up. They can feel it, and they know what it is. We refer to it as emotional throw up. Not so different from throwing up food, it's the body's way of releasing what it doesn't need. It really doesn't matter what it's from, and it's probably not one thing. Most likely it's a number of issues, disappointments, or frustrations that have built up over time. The body knows when it's ready to rid itself of the discomfort.

All children need a safe space to release, a place where they can cry at the top of their lungs and not be told to calm down. A place where they can shed tears and not be told to hurry up. A place where they can let go and still be validated and loved. Allowing children to release their emotions builds trust. Because they feel safe doing so, our relationship with them is deepened.

Children "throw up" emotions because they are wise enough to listen to their bodies. Adults, on the other hand, tend to think sadness and anger are unacceptable, a display of weakness; so they stuff their emotions down and pretend they doesn't exist. Then the suppressed emotion emerges as road rage, fights with coworkers, angry Facebook posts, or is taken out on a significant other or their children.

When I talk about emotional "throw up" in my classes or presentations, one or more parents will usually say, "That would never happen in my house. My child would never do what your kids do. They don't realize that they need to release."

My response is, "Teach them." Help them understand how emotions build up and how they need to be released. Make this a normal discussion in your household. Make it okay to emotionally throw up every once in a while.

I'm not talking about giving children permission to hit or harm others. This isn't about reacting emotionally, snapping like an alligator. It isn't about venting rage. I'm talking about creating some normalcy around crying, talking, and other safe ways to let go of pent-up emotion.

Our children need us to let them know we feel both sad and mad sometimes, and they need to see how we deal with these emotions safely. This is important not only for individual emotional health, but also for a family's emotional well-being. It's about having our children accept all aspects of themselves, even the parts that aren't so pretty and we all try to pretend we don't have.

I know Skylar would prefer to be happy, or at least calm, in the mornings. But on this particular morning, she needed to throw up. She needed to let go of discomfort in a safe way and safe place. So she sat on her dad's lap for a full ten minutes, wailing and screaming while hugging her dad tightly. When she was done, she rested, then returned to her chair.

"Didn't that feel good?" I asked. "I'm so glad you got that out."

She nodded, smiled, and said, "Can I please have a waffle now?"

31

Carrying negative emotions

AFTER PICKING UP MY DAUGHTERS from school, I was sitting at a stop sign. When it was my turn to go, I proceeded through the intersection. Unfortunately, the truck to the left of me believed it was his turn, and he almost hit the side of my car.

"Almost" is the key word. We both stopped abruptly, avoiding an accident.

But whoa! Was he mad. He pounded his fists on the steering wheel, gave me the finger, and yelled as if I could actually hear what he was saying through our closed side windows. I gave him a quick wave and drove away.

However, the emotion I felt from his rudeness didn't go away. I was left feeling frustrated and fearful.

It was then that the stories began to swirl in my head: *It was my turn. I have three little girls in this car! What if he hit me? How dare he yell at me? It was his fault, not mine.*

About five blocks later, I wanted to let it go. I was so pissed off that my heartbeat was actually erratic. I also realized the stories I was telling myself were completely unnecessary, since the incident was long over and they had no power to affect it.

Then a story about ducks came floating into my mind from

Eckhart Tolle's book *A New Earth*. When ducks clash and get into a tiff, they argue with each other by quacking loudly, then swim off and flap away the unpleasant energy generated by the incident. After releasing the negative energy, they don't swim over to other ducks to share their sob story. Neither do they take out their frustration on their duck family. They just flap, then peacefully carry on with what they were doing before the altercation occurred.

The truck incident upset me, but why did I need to carry it into my day by talking about it incessantly and making up stories in my mind about what could have happened?

Instead of sticking with my stories, I started breathing, which for me is a good way of releasing. I also moved my head and shoulders about as I told myself, "Shake it off, shake it off." By the time I arrived home, my head was tingling and I knew the emotion had been released.

I was back. I didn't even tell my husband, since I had no need to.

Life being what it is, I had yet another opportunity to deal with strong emotion shortly thereafter as I dropped my girls off at school. No sooner had we pulled up at the curb than Camryn realized she had forgotten her backpack. Since she couldn't fathom going into class without it, she decided she didn't want to go to school. Starting to cry, she was soon beside herself.

What to do?

"Breathe, just breathe," I told myself.

I decided to send Jacey into school, while Camryn and I got back into the car. "You know your backpack is your responsibility, right?" I reminded her.

"I know," she said.

I don't like backtracking, so naturally I was frustrated and annoyed. We drove home in silence.

When we arrived back at the school, backpack in tow, Cam was quiet, clearly feeling bad. I didn't feel very good either. Getting out of the car, I said, "It's time to shake it off. Let's move." We started jumping around in front of the school, doing yoga moves and a few dance moves. I can't imagine what people were thinking if they happened to be watching us. We finished with a deep inhale, followed by an exhale, then held hands as we walked up to the entrance. I gave Camryn a kiss, and she smiled. I told her I'd see her at 3:00. As I drove away, I felt powerful.

I can't control what other people say or do. I can't even control the arising of my emotions. They are a normal part of being human, and they show up for a reason. But once the emotion has been fully felt, I can let it go. The incident is already over, and the emotion that accompanied it has nothing to do with the present moment.

Negative emotion is just that—an emotion. It's meant to be felt, worked through, and let go. Holding onto it only creates heaviness and drama, two things I can definitely do without. I'd rather reach for my inner duck, feel it, shake it off, and swim away in peace.

32

What's the difference between happiness and joy?

Happiness is a gift from a friend or a kiss from a child. Joy is feeling love for someone, and noticing when someone loves us.

Happiness is a day when things are going really well. Joy is finding a way to laugh when things become scary, or smiling at someone on the street even when we are feeling heavy.

Happiness is a good beer and a great pizza. Joy is realizing we have access to food and water, all the time.

Happiness is feeling the sunshine on a beautiful day. Joy is knowing that the sun is always there, even when it's cloudy.

Happiness is winning an award or getting a raise. Joy is waking up every morning and doing what you love.

Happiness comes and goes. Joy comes and goes, but it's *always* a choice.

Happiness is an emotion, and emotions naturally change. Joy is realizing, regardless of how we are feeling, that we are okay, and that things are going to be okay.

Happiness comes from things working out the way we planned. Joy is knowing that the plan is bigger than our immediate desires.

Happiness usually comes from external circumstance. Joy comes from inside, from being grateful and noticing what's working.

Happiness is a wish. Joy is a practice.

Happiness can be surface. Joy runs deep.

Appreciate happiness. Live joy.

Are you enjoying your joy, or pushing it away?

JOY IS ALWAYS AROUND US, ever present, everywhere. But we've been trained not to take it in. Worse, we've learned to push it away.

Why? For self-protection. We're afraid to let ourselves be *too* happy, or the proverbial other shoe may drop. We don't want to be too joyful, lest we find ourselves unprepared for the next disaster. After all, if we let ourselves feel joy, how will we cope with the shift to the emotional pain, frustration, and disappointment we tell ourselves inevitably follow?

We stay just a little low so that we don't have to experience the fluctuation of the extremes of feeling.

The problem is, choosing not to feel joy doesn't protect us from pain. Pretending not to care doesn't keep us from caring. Besides, our job on earth is to experience joy, appreciate our time here, enjoy the beauty. Otherwise, why are we here? To suffer? I don't think so. Yes, any human life experiences an array of emotion, including pain, fear, disappointment, grief, excitement, surprise. But they are emotions, not *who we are.*

The more we take in life's joy, the more we enjoy our stay here.

EMOTION
Cathy Cassani Adams, LCSW, CPC, CYT

We have a limited stay on this earth. Why waste it by not enjoying it? I realize you already know this, but it's something all of us need reminding of. Because no matter that it sounds cliché, it's true.

When do we think we are supposed to start enjoying life? We tell our kids to buckle down, focus more on doing than being, focus more on work rather than play. Why? Because we believe this will help them be "happy." Well, aren't most of us still doing this? We're buckling down, focusing more on doing than being, working more than playing. When does it end and the "happy" part arrive?

How about now?

This moment is *it*, the only thing that's real. If this moment isn't working for you, it's your responsibility to make a change, seek support, and have faith in finding something better. It won't just happen—it takes making a decision. You can *choose* to feel the joy.

To begin down this path, notice when something feels good, acknowledge it, and take it in. Maybe it's a loving moment with your partner, a fun moment with your children, something fulfilling at work, or simply enjoying nature. Breathe it in instead of pushing it away. Don't treat it as if it's a fluke, not true, or not lasting. *Take it*, realizing it's yours to keep.

Again, you may want to push it away to protect yourself, but question that. For example, you're having a really great day and the first thing you think is, "Uh oh, what's going to go wrong...something has to go wrong." What is that? It's not true. It's just a story of protection.

Here are some of the other unhelpful stories we tell ourselves:

1. I have one healthy child, so most likely the next one won't be.

2. I love my family, so there's no way I can love my work, too. That's just too much (or vice versa).

3. We had a good time last year, but there's no way we can have such a good time again.

4. Things feel great now, but I know something's around the corner.

5. Two of my kids are really well behaved, so there's no way the third one will be, too.

6. This year was great, so that must mean that next year will suck.

7. I feel so good right now, but I know I don't deserve it.

8. This is too good to be true.

9. I'm much more comfortable when things are going wrong; I know how to handle that.

10. I've already achieved one dream. I don't want to get greedy and ask for more.

Are you getting the point? We feel joy, and we push it away as if it was a fluke, or undeserved, or only a momentary thing before everything comes crashing down. Instead of enjoying the joy, it becomes almost a burden because in our mind it signifies something "bad" is on its way. I realize this is because we don't want to be vulnerable, don't want to set ourselves up for disaster. But the truth is that choosing joy doesn't set you up, any more than choosing not to feel joy protects you. It just numbs you.

No amount of preparation can keep you from experiencing

the emotion of life's many twists and turns. When trauma comes, you deal with it in that moment.

For example, you can't be prepared for the experience of birth. Yes, you can take a class, have a doula, practice hypno-birthing. But nobody could have truly prepared me for the physical and emotional experience giving birth turned out to be.

Neither can you be prepared for what it means to be a parent. You can have the diapers and clothes ready, but the emotional experience is a moment-by-moment learning process.

When it comes to someone's death, you can have paperwork in order and the various issues involved worked out, but the emotional experience of grief can only be experienced in the moment, and there's no way to skip over it.

Disasters, natural or otherwise, aren't something you can be prepared for, beyond having extra food and water available. You can't plan for every contingency, and you can't know what might lie around the corner. Sometimes things just happen. When they do, your instinct and survival skills take over, and you handle the situation in a state of awareness.

Being anxious and joyless doesn't help. It only stifles your ability to respond to situations in the moment. It also keeps you in a perpetual state of preparation rather than living each day at a time.

The truth is that it's often more difficult to sit in love and joy than it is in pain, mostly because joy feels too big, too real, too raw. Why does it feel this way? Because it's evoking something from our past. When we were young, the natural joy we knew was suppressed by family, society, and the educational system. Today, whenever we feel joy, it reawakens the trauma we experienced as we were forced to abandon our joyful self in favor of social norms. So we shut it off, just like we learned to do when we were little.

For this reason, living joyfully is something we have to practice. When you're experiencing a joyful moment, take a deep breath and take it in. Embrace it and appreciate it as one of the many gifts of being alive. It won't make you weak or slow. On the contrary, it will empower you. It will take you out of your head and into your heart. Then when issues arise—when you are grieving, in pain, or disappointed—you will be stronger and more able to deal with what you're going through. You'll have a reserve of energy to pull from, greater clarity, and the imagination you require to address the situation in an effective, heart-centered way.

You will have a better perspective on life, with an appreciation for the fact that to be here on earth involves a subtle interplay of light and dark. You can't control it, but you can learn to move with its flow and appreciate all the good things along the way.

What do you want for your kids? Do you want them to breathe in the joy of life, or to focus on doom and gloom because they feel unworthy of the good?

They learn by watching how you live. When you bask in your joy, it gives them permission to do the same.

EMOTION
Cathy Cassani Adams, LCSW, CPC, CYT

Where joy really comes from

I PICKED UP MY DAUGHTER from Kindergarten and she said, "I just feel so like me today. I love feeling like me." As we walked to the car, she held my hand, skipped, and hummed.

On this particular day, she was wearing hand-me-downs from her sisters, barrettes she'd found under her bed, and bright blue shoes. We didn't have any planned outings or a fun lunch date. There were no special stars on her papers, no birthday invitations in her folder, and she'd been given no special job.

Nothing out of the ordinary was happening around her, and yet she felt good in her skin, good being herself.

This is the joy we tend to lose touch with as we grow. We become so focused on the doing things, and so keen to ensure everybody knows what we're doing, that we crowd out the joy that's bedrock to our being.

It's one thing to choose what feels good. But when our only intention is to enhance other people's perception of us, we're going down a path that can't fulfill us—a path over which we actually have no control, since we can't determine another person's response. The only thing we can control is our own inner feeling: whether or not we like ourselves.

Money can't buy good feelings. And while another person's feelings about us may flatter us, the desire for praise and popularity is insatiable and offers only a short-lived high.

The really important questions are, "How do I feel about being me? Do I really know myself? Can I feel what I am? Do I pay attention to what I've been given? Do I offer myself the love I know all humans deserve?"

At one time, we all knew inner joy. Before people told us to be different. Before we learned to compare and compete. Before we decided others had it better.

Joy doesn't come from stuff or constant productivity. It springs from a quiet and deep inner acceptance and appreciation of who we are—a feeling of fullness, of adequacy, of knowing that who we are is good.

On this particular day, I took my daughter's picture, framed it, and set it on her dresser. I wanted her to remember how joy feels.

Or perhaps I took the picture for me—so that I can remember where joy really comes from.

EMOTION
Cathy Cassani Adams, LCSW, CPC, CYT

Raising emotionally intelligent boys:
why we need to let our sons feel

WHEN MY OLDEST ENTERED fifth grade, it felt like a milestone. Teetering between childhood and preadolescence, fifth grade is an ideal time to focus on self-understanding, emotional expression, body image, and stress reduction. In other words, basically everything we adults are still working on!

This is a moment in a young person's life when peers become more important and pressures become more common. To address this, my husband and I created a fifth-grade self-awareness curriculum entitled *Be U*. It's designed for twenty kids—ten girls and ten boys. In our first run with this program, it required only a few simple emails to fill the ten spots for girls. The class was scheduled for the fall, and we even had to start a waiting list for girls who wanted to take the class in the spring.

In contrast, nobody signed up their fifth-grade boys.

Initially we figured it was because we have three daughters, so naturally we know more families with girls. We felt that when we opened it to the public, the spots would fill. Although more and more girls wanted in, only a few emails trickled in from parents with boys. The difference between parents wanting their girls to participate and parents wanting their boys to participate was extreme.

The phenomenon speaks to a major issue in our society, which is our inability to grasp the importance of male emotional awareness. Even using the words "male" and "emotional" in the same sentence causes some to roll their eyes.

The fact is that boys struggle with many of the same issues as girls. They get hurt by others, become victims of bullying, experience body image issues, and feel tremendous pressure to compete and be the "best." They also have the extra pressure of having to pretend they aren't scared or sad when they face challenges.

Our culture raises boys to believe they need to be competitive, powerful, brave, and strong. These are positive traits when they are balanced with emotional awareness. But without emotional awareness, such traits show up as aggression, violence, greed—all symptoms of disconnection from other people, our fellow creatures on the planet, and the planet itself. The flip side of this is that a lack of emotional awareness can lead to depression, self-harm, and even suicide.

It's imperative that boys grow up to have a healthy emotional life so that their masculinity is tempered with compassion. For this to happen, they need their feelings to be acknowledged and respected. Currently, many boys feel unheard, which causes them to be angry, since anger is just a second-tier emotion to sadness, embarrassment, or any other uncomfortable or unacknowledged feeling.

Many boys are brought up to believe that feelings are bad, and too often squelching emotions is considered to be the masculine thing to do. Emotion is looked upon as feminine, and no boy wants to be called a "girl," which would mean they are perceived as weak—a perception of females that's itself tragic. So as not to be called a "sissy," boys learn to numb their feelings, the consequence of which is that they live in a disconnected state.

It's this disconnection that shows up as an inability to honor women, to connect with male friends over anything but sports and business, and to value the need for power and money over the common good.

It's because they are emotionally stunted that males become fixated on competition, being the best, and making money. They prize getting ahead because they have a need to prove they are worthy, since they were never made to feel worthy in themselves. In the process, males miss out on the joy that can be found in their daily experiences. Because they feel too disconnected, too numb to notice what's working in their lives quite apart from having to prove themselves, they can't feel gratitude.

Many men have no clue how to listen to and understand other people's feelings because nobody took the time to understand their feelings. In contrast, a boy who understands his inner workings has the capacity to connect and to feel empowered from within. He grows up to use his strengths to give back to society. He feels the joy of a loving relationship, as well as the relief of being real instead of putting on a show.

We need this kind of male leadership. We need more males who know how to listen to others, respect other people's opinions, tolerate differences, and understand what it takes to work as a team. Although I know there are many emotionally intelligent males, and I'm lucky to know some of them, this needs to become the dominant mode for all men. However, for this to become a reality, our society has a lot of work to do. We owe our boys more than we are presently offering them.

It's time to let go of our stereotypes and start opening up to the idea that, regardless of gender, we all need emotional awareness. We all need to be allowed to cry and be held, to experience self-love, to feel connected, and to speak from the heart.

36

Talking to students about emotional awareness

RECENTLY I TALKED TO MY college students about mindfulness. The class is an Introduction to Social Work, and the focus that particular day was on noticing our thoughts, questioning the validity of these thoughts, and creating space between ourselves and our thoughts.

There were a lot of blank stares, and I realize some of my students think I'm wacky. Yet I know how important this information is for their lives. Besides, this wasn't my first day of blank stares. We've covered self-love, personal awareness, laughter, forgiveness, taking responsibility, and practicing compassion. The core of the curriculum is self-understanding, because how can a student become an effective social worker if they don't know who they are? How can they help others heal if they don't know what it takes to heal or what healing feels like?

Sometimes, when class is over, I sit down and feel crazy. Sometimes I shake a little or feel lightheaded. This is something that also tends to happen following a parenting presentation, when I push the "publish" button on a blog, or after my husband and I tape a radio show.

The crazy feeling usually starts with something like, "What

are you talking about?" and ends with, "Who do you think you are?"

The funny thing is that when I am talking, lecturing, or writing, I don't feel crazy. I'm just going with the flow and trusting what comes. Were you to ask me to repeat what I just said, or figure out where a statement came from, I usually couldn't. Yet when it comes out, it feels not only congruent but loving.

Age and experience have taught me I'll often feel crazy, but that the crazy sensation isn't actually me. It's just a big wad of fear and worry, coupled with old beliefs that still want a voice. My best defense in these moments is a combination of humor and questions.

Humor helps me disarm the negativity with some gentle self-effacing agreement. "Yes, your students think you're nuts—roll with it." Questioning allows me to disconnect from those thoughts that try to tell me what I feel and teach isn't correct—that who I am and what I have to share isn't valid.

What I know for sure and want my students to know is that what we feel and who we are is both valuable and important.

Do we recognize our importance, and do we practice being true to ourselves? Do we do what feels right, or do we do what's expected? Do we say what we know could really help, or do we say what everybody agrees with because it's more palatable?

It comes down to whether we allow ourselves to be seen or whether we blend in to stay safe. We all feel like blending once in a while—that's normal. But when we blend too much, we lose touch with what feels right, lose touch with our individual nature, and end up feeling less than whole. And when we don't feel whole, it's difficult to offer ourselves to others—difficult to be great in our profession, our parenting, our studies.

EMOTION

Cathy Cassani Adams, LCSW, CPC, CYT

How can we enjoy what we do when we don't know who we are and what we have to offer?

While it's important for my social work students to graduate from my class knowing about Jane Addams, social work theory, and social class, it's equally important they leave considering and contemplating their own worthiness.

Then, when as future social workers and citizens of the world they face challenges and feel crazy sometimes, maybe they'll question the crazy feeling rather than believe they are somehow flawed. Perhaps they'll question the thoughts that disconnect them from what feels right and true. They may even find some humor in it all, maintain their balance, and realize they have the tools to be of service to others, while at the same time enjoying their lives.

37

Crying is real, crying is strong

I USED TO BE UNCOMFORTABLE in emotional movies because I'm a crier. In a movie, or when witnessing an act of kindness or hearing a touching story, I used to hold my breath, wipe my eyes quickly, or blink fast—whatever was required to retain my composure.

For some reason, I've always been easily moved. I spent a lot of my childhood and early adulthood fighting back tears or finding the nearest bathroom so that I could cry without anyone seeing me.

For the last several years, I've traded bathroom stalls for allowing. Allowing my tears, allowing my emotional expression, allowing myself to do whatever I need to do. By allowing, I've learned so much about tears, especially the way they can heal. I've discovered so much about emotions and how they allow us to process our experience of the world.

An emotional response to something is our system's way of working through it, allowing it to hit our heart, then recovering from the often intense experience. Such a response is a deeply present-moment experience, a "stop and feel" situation. Once felt, tears allow us move forward with lightness.

To swallow our tears or suppress our emotions is to stifle reality. It's a way of shutting off, which of course is a pretense. We prevent the body from doing what it naturally knows it needs to do. So although I used to think of my ability to "hold it in" as an essential defense, now I view it as a delay or even flat-out denial of feeling.

Today I recognize that feelings are a gift, and crying a natural tool.

Of course, there's a need for balance, so I'm more reserved with my tears when teaching, counseling, and presenting. But when it comes to life in my home, I let them loose. Thankfully my husband doesn't try to stop me or distract me, but is usually quiet. Resting his hand on my leg, he trusts my ability to process.

My daughters know their mom is a crier, even though in the early days I used to quickly wipe my eyes, give an excuse for my emotion, or walk away so that they couldn't see. Now I cry openly. When my girls look at me, I look them in the eye. Sometimes I even smile so that they know I trust myself. I don't make excuses for my emotion and don't act ashamed. If I need space, I ask for it; and when I return, I let them know I'm better, because I do feel better when I cry.

It's when I have an emotional experience that I feel most real. Something touches my heart, and I feel connected. I don't want to stifle it, and I don't want to teach my girls how to stifle it.

The best part of tears is that I often end up laughing. Somehow tears and laughter get intertwined, especially when I'm having a big cry. It's a reminder of how closely joy and sadness are linked, and of how light and dark go hand in hand. The more I feel and show my tears, the more profound my joy. The more I experience something as difficult, the more grateful and present I am for the calm that follows.

Though I can still imagine myself as a child, hiding somewhere, swallowing my feelings, feeling weak because I couldn't "control" my emotions, today I just cry. I cry with people who are crying. I cry when I experience loss. I cry when I feel tremendous happiness and gratitude. I don't feel compelled to hide anymore. I grab a Kleenex, make eye contact, breathe, and smile.

It feels nothing but real, nothing but strong.

Why do risk-takers take risks?

MY DEFINITION OF RISK-TAKER may be different than yours. I don't jump out of planes. I'm not a world traveler. I don't have any tattoos or piercings beyond the basic holes in my earlobes. And for some reason, my wardrobe is filled with a lot of gray and black (I'm working on this one). Yet I definitely believe in *emotional* risk-taking, by which I mean noticing myself on a daily basis—my challenges, my issues, my triggers. It's not always pretty, but I notice. I watch myself closely.

When I feel fear, anxiety, defensiveness, envy—all the normal human emotions—my first question is, "Why?"

By "why," I mean things like what am I afraid of? What do I think it means? Where does it all stem from?

Usually the answer goes something like this: I'm afraid of being rejected, afraid that who I am is wrong, afraid I'll be alone.

Yikes, and yikes! But that's usually the bottom-line truth for me.

At the same time, I know it's not "the truth" at all. These are just old wounds—pain that started as love and got all tangled up in misperception and misunderstanding somewhere along the way. Then the love became fear. Fear that who I am isn't good enough. Fear of being disconnected.

We humans need connection. We want to feel connected to ourselves and to others. Our cry is, "See me, hear me, love me, and let me do the same for you!" Though sometimes, when we're feeling disconnected, we pretend we don't care. We pretend it doesn't matter, pretend it's somebody else's fault. Pretend, pretend, pretend.

Or, we want the connection so badly, we pretend to be someone we aren't, say things we don't believe, say yes to things we don't want to do, pretend social perception is more important than self-respect.

Pretending is so painful. It squashes what's real, ruins our moments, gives away our power. This is what we do when we don't watch ourselves closely. This is what we do when we are moving through life on autopilot.

We have to be brave enough to take risks, and we have to trust that these risks will pay off. Not because everyone will like it, or because it's always easy, or because mistakes will never be made. Rather, risking being ourselves pays off because we feel good inside. We feel calm, full, and intact, rather than empty.

That "hole" you feel inside? That "thing" you think is missing? That's just the holy-thing that's trying to remind you to be yourself.

Yourself is trying to help yourself.

When you risk in order to be yourself, you not only feel good, but people enjoy your presence. They may not have words for why they enjoy your presence; they just feel good when they are around you. So while it's true that some may no longer "get" you, the ones who do get you will like you even more.

Why do risk-takers take risks? Because there's a natural high that comes with risk-taking—just ask those who race cars or jump off cliffs. In a similar way, there's a natural high that comes from being open, taking responsibility, and telling the truth about how we feel or who we are in any given moment. These are the risks we fear most. But when taken, we experience true connection and the natural high of being alive.

COMMUNICATION

*Courage is what it takes to stand up and speak;
it's also what it takes to sit down and listen.*

WINSTON CHURCHILL

Helping kids by talking less, accepting more

WE WANT OUR CHILDREN to come to us when they are struggling. We want them to know we are a resource when they are confused. We want them to trust that we are always available when life gets them down.

The problem is that when they come to us, we tend to talk too much. Instead of being a safe haven, we teach. Rather than being an understanding presence, we lecture.

Don't worry, you aren't alone in this; I struggle with it, too. I've had to remove the words "teachable moment" from my vocabulary because I was finding way too many of them. I always felt like I had something important to say. But my professional and personal experience show me that kids need less talking and more listening. They need fewer lectures, less judgment, and more unwavering support.

In the moment of sharing, they are highly vulnerable. They need to feel safe with the decision to talk to us. They need to know our first instinct is unconditional love.

We want to guide our children and tell them how to make life easier, but the truth is that mistakes and challenges are necessary and normal. We hope to share lessons that inspire conscientious decisions, but in the end our children learn by making a number of poor choices.

It's important to understand that children learn by watching how we live, not from what we say. So while we are focused on telling them something, they are observing our choices, watching the way we treat ourselves, and paying attention to how we deal with challenges.

For this reason, instead of focusing on words, we need to demonstrate what we want to teach. If we want our children to be less anxious, we need to model what this looks like. When we have difficulty modeling appropriate behavior, we need to acknowledge this, ask for forgiveness, and find the courage to try again.

In the meantime, as we work on our actions, we can practice being quieter and less judgmental when our children come to us for help. They usually just want to share their experience so that they can move on. Even more importantly, they want to know we are present when they feel overwhelmed, and that we can momentarily set aside our urge to teach, and instead listen, empathize, and accept.

40

Learning to listen to our kids

A LOT OF MY TIME IS SPENT listening to my girls. They tell stories, ask questions, or just release a stream of consciousness with me present.

Sometimes I repeat back what they say: "That upset you, huh?" Or I respond with encouragement: "Absolutely, that makes sense."

At other times I ask simple questions so that they know I'm listening: "Wow. Then what happened?" I do a lot of head nodding, and sometimes I utter the occasional "Oh," "Hmm," or "Ahh."

While this seems like no big deal, just a regular part of a regular day, I learned that it's actually a very big deal. You see, it's what teaches my daughters they have a safe place to share. They understand home to be a loving space in which they can discuss whatever is most meaningful to them and process it in a secure environment.

I do my best to just listen instead of offering unsolicited advice. This isn't always the case, since I may share a lesson or two. But when I do so, I try to be thoughtful before I speak. Judgment, criticism, and even an opinion have a way of ruining a meaningful conversation.

Because my girls get so much redirection during the day—from me, teachers, coaches—sometimes they just need an opportunity to release without being evaluated. My intention is to let them say what they need to say, in whatever way they need to say it.

Being a good listener can be tiring, and I don't always have enough energy or space in my own day to be present and engaged. This is especially true when the questions tax my brain, such as, "Mom, why does the wind blow?" or, "Mom, what's that thing that does that thing to the thing?" This is reason enough for me to carve out time for myself. I like to spend my early mornings in quiet, as well as taking an hour in the afternoon to do my own thing. I find this essential if I'm really going to hear my kids.

Then there are times when it's just one of those days. There's no time for self-care, I'm too tired, or I have too much to do. On such days, I have to let the girls know I'm not up to the task of being a good listener because I'm too overwhelmed with my own stuff. Instead, I may suggest a show or book together—or if I'm really lucky, a nap together.

As parents, we tend to feel guilty about what we aren't doing for our children or what we aren't giving them. We expend energy feeling bad about things we can't afford, trips we can't take, or the class we couldn't get them into.

I think children's needs are simpler. They just want to be seen and heard—things that require us to simply put the phone down, stop cleaning the kitchen, and look them in the eye. We can sit across from them in a chair, listen intently, and maybe grab their hand so that they know we are really there.

Yes, we are busy, and there are many things during the day

that demand our time and energy. As parents, it's our job to be conscious of what's truly important. Many things *seem* important, and other people like to tell us what's important. But I've learned that nothing is as important as the story my daughter is about to tell me. She's sharing her life with me.

When I listen, I share my love with her.

COMMUNICATION

Cathy Cassani Adams, LCSW, CPC, CYT

41

Don't pretend, just communicate

ONE MORNING, I totally rushed my daughter. Todd was traveling and I had to teach a class at 8:30. From the moment she got up, I was moving her along.

Because it's her nature to observe, my daughter moves slowly and isn't at all comfortable doing things quickly. For her to eat requires time. She also needs time to figure out what she's going to wear. And she has to have time to just space out. Rushing her this particular morning made me uncomfortable.

My problem was that I wanted to be on time for my class. My other two were already in the car, but this one was taking a while to get there. Feeling frustrated, I took several deep breaths and tried to stay quiet.

Finally, my agitation got the better of me and I started bombarding her with questions. "Why don't you pick out your clothes at night?" I demanded. "Why does it take you so long to eat your breakfast?"

She had heard these things before. Consequently, she was quiet. When I dropped her off at school, her energy was low. It wasn't the greatest way to start a morning.

As I drove to my class, I pondered how I could have handled

things differently. Yes, I needed to leave on time. But was there a different way to handle this situation, a better way to motivate her?

When I picked her up from school, it seemed she had forgotten all about it. But I didn't want to sweep this issue under the rug and pretend that this morning didn't happen. Pretending may seem easier, but it eats away at the relationship, eventually becoming a heavy burden that generates tension and frustration. Over time, it's hard to remember how the frustration began.

As the parent, the adult in the situation, do we pretend nothing's wrong? Or do we foster openness by engaging in conversation? I decided it was my responsibility to take the lead and engage my daughter in communication.

I want to interject that it's never too late to start a conversation, whether something happened only recently, a week ago, or even a long time ago. Unresolved issues need to be brought up and discussed in a manner that allows both people to be heard, both to be validated, both to be respected.

Although it can be uncomfortable to initiate these conversations, we must do it anyway.

After allowing my daughter space to relax, I asked her to lie down with me so that we could talk. Then I explained, "I didn't like the way I felt when I dropped you off this morning. I want to leave you at school feeling good, not low. So, how can we make the mornings smoother? How can we do things differently?"

At first she was hesitant to respond, but then some ideas started to flow. It may be that none of them were actually new. However, finding a solution was only part of the reason I wanted to have this conversation. My main objective was that we be real with each other. She needed to hear my perspective, and I needed to hear hers. Even if we couldn't find a solution immediately, at least we opened up a discussion.

When we are real, we don't feed passive-aggressive behavior on either of our parts, and we don't resort to guilt-tripping. As we continue to be real with each other, we gradually learn together, eventually coming up with a win-win solution.

42

Finding a safe space to unravel untruths

WHEN CAMRYN AND SKYLAR walked in the front door, immediately Camryn said, "Skylar fed the dog sand, but he didn't die yet."

I stopped what I was doing and said, "Would you run that by me again?"

"Skylar had sand in her hand, and a dog licked it," she explained. It turned out that a little girl they were playing with said her dad told her that if a dog ate sand, it would die.

As Camryn shared the story, Skylar began to cry, insisting, "Don't talk about it. Don't say it!"

I immediately sat down on the floor and asked both of them to join me. Putting my arms around them, I promised them none of it was true. Although I don't know much about dogs, I do know their bodies can tolerate licking a little girl's hand with sand in it.

When Skylar continued to cry, releasing the anxiety she had carried for that short amount of time, I reassured her, "You did nothing wrong. The dog is fine. What you were told isn't true." As we all rocked back and forth, I promised her over and over that all was well.

This small simple untruth could have stayed with my kids, but Camryn's decision to share allowed it to unravel before it became embedded as a belief. Not just the part about a dog eating sand, but that they participated in an event that could have led to a dog's death. Maybe it wouldn't have affected them at all. On the other hand, it could have shown up as a fear of dogs. They might also tell themselves they aren't trustworthy enough to handle animals. Who knows?

As I sat there thinking through these "what ifs," I also accepted the fact I can't protect my children from every untruth they hear. They will encounter so many in their lifetime, and there's not a thing I can do to prevent it. From little matters to major issues, they will hear and experience things that scare them, and I won't be there to unravel all of it.

The incident made me more aware of how important it is for my children to feel comfortable sharing absolutely anything with me—and how essential it is that I listen without judging. Children thrive when we create an environment in which any question can be asked, any mistake revealed, without a long lecture, guilt tripping, or any kind of threat.

I also realized how important it is for me to be quiet around my children instead of constantly talking. In this way, I create the space for them to share. Having a calm house allows the girls to come home to peace when they feel rattled.

Though I can't control what my children hear and what scares them, I can offer myself to them. Not by prodding them with questions or holding onto them too tightly to "keep them safe," but by letting go, trusting them, and having open arms and ears when they return. They need me to look them in the eye and smile at them on a daily basis, so that they know I see and love them.

LIVING WHAT YOU WANT YOUR KIDS TO LEARN
Cathy Cassani Adams, LCSW, CPC, CYT

I try my best to be with my children during their most open and vulnerable times, such as right before bed and first thing in the morning. It helps for me to quietly lie down with them so that they can share their fears, observations, and worries. I want them to know they can release these things from their bodies, and I will listen, support, and love them.

I never want them to endure discomfort or fear because they're worried I'll think less of them if they don't keep something to themselves. They need to know in their deepest being that no matter what happens, love will always be a constant in our conversations—a truth that can't be taught with just words but is learned only by experiencing it consistently.

Part of my responsibility toward my children is to work through my own untruths, so many of them ridiculously old, and clear out space so that I have the room, patience, and clarity to handle whatever my kids need to share.

As I was thinking all this through, Skylar stopped crying and I stopped rocking. Looking both girls in the eye, I held their hands and said, "If you are ever afraid, ever hear something that makes your insides hurt, ever question something you've done, or think of yourself as bad, please come talk to me, your dad, or somebody else you trust. Don't carry the burden on your own. Come home and let it go."

They nodded and ran outside, back to the real world, while I remained on the kitchen floor and had a brief cry. I felt the untruths I used to carry as a child, and I also felt relieved I could support my girls through this one. At the same time, I felt scared that at some point in the future they would make the decision not to share—that their fear would be greater than their trust.

It was soothing to know that the best thing I can do for my family is know myself. I can release my fears, let go of my untruths, and find my own personal safety. I can love myself so that I can be available, patient, open, calm, and loving for them. That's the energy I want them to feel when they walk through the door. That's the kind of security I want to provide.

43

"Please don't look at me, please don't talk to me"

I HAD JUST FINISHED having lunch with my almost-four-year-old daughter. When we sat down to eat, the first thing she said was, "Please don't look at me, and please don't talk to me."

"Oh," I responded, "I was hoping to talk with you over lunch today."

"I don't want to," she asserted.

"Okay," I agreed. So we sat in silence. Occasionally I noticed her glancing at me, but I just continued to eat, enjoying my food, enjoying the peace.

After about fifteen minutes she said, "Do you know that Camryn likes jelly?" And then our conversation began.

As we drove away from the restaurant, I reflected on our last thirty-five minutes. At first I had been taken aback by my daughter's request. Then I wondered why I was taken aback. Surely it's a good thing to ask for space, peace, and quiet?

Naturally, the mom in me wanted to explain why my daughter's choice not to talk to me might be offensive. Yet the truth is, it wasn't offensive. Besides, at that moment her emotional need seemed a lot more important than teaching her yet another way to please other people. I appreciate that my daughter let me know what she needed—and what she needed was space. She didn't want all the questions like at school, or when she's at her friend's house, or when she's with her sisters. She wanted to sit and not be "on."

I can so relate.

This might be a difficult request in another setting, such as with people she doesn't know well. But I can handle it. And I admire it.

44

The problem with "yeah, but"

SOMETIMES WHEN I ANSWER a question, I notice the one who asked it has stopped listening.

Midway through my response I feel a shift in the individual. I sense I'm about to hear two familiar words we all tend to use from time to time: "Yeah, but."

Yeah, I hear what you're saying, but that won't work for me because....

Yeah, that's a good idea, but I can't do that because....

Yeah, I hear you, but my situation is completely different.....

I find this to be a common response whenever I offer a new parenting or self-care solution, share another way to view misbehavior or discipline, or suggest feeling emotions and allowing children to share emotions. I usually notice a shaking of the head, along with a look that says, *Yeah, that may work for you, but....* This is followed by a list of the challenges that stand in the way of real change.

At some point or other, all of us "Yeah, but" our way through a conversation. It's a way of being protective of the way we look at things, the choices we make, and our reasons for why we do things the way we do them. We're saying in effect, "All doable options have been explored. Our circumstances are different. You can't possibly understand my unique situation."

There is truth to this. It *is* impossible to fully comprehend another's life experiences. At the same time, real growth depends on our ability to be open to new possibilities. It's like the analogy of the empty cup. If we truly seek to learn, we must arrive with our cup empty so that there's room to take in something new. So many of us show up with great questions, but we are unable to hear the answers because our cup is spilling over with what we already believe to be true. There's simply no room for new insight.

I confess there are aspects of my personal and professional life in which I tend to carry a full cup of knowledge and experiences. I have moments when I believe I've heard and seen it all. But of course, this isn't true. Quite the opposite. The older I become, the more I realize how much I don't know. So I make it a practice to be attentive. Not just in everyday situations, but also in areas outside my comfort zone. I find something that intrigues me, usually something I have let go of at some point in my life, and I attempt to relearn.

My current learning curve involves tap dancing. Believe me, I'm the beginner of the beginners in the beginners' class. This means I have to listen intently, watch the others around me closely, and be fully engaged in the learning process. In this situation, my cup is big-time empty—something that isn't always comfortable, requiring me to check my ego at the door.

But it's also pretty great, because I feel like a kid experiencing something new. In other words, I'm truly present in what I'm doing; I'm fully connected and fully engaged. It inspires me to bring this type of studentship into my everyday life, especially in those areas in which I imagine I know it all.

Like when my husband wants to share something I think I already know. I want so badly to "Yeah, but him." But as in dance, I check my ego at the door and practice good studentship. I make an effort to empty my cup, soften my rigidity, and really listen. Whenever I succeed in this, I feel him soften too, since he realizes I'm not competing with him. I don't need to be right, don't need to win—and neither does he. It's then that we begin to hear and learn from each other.

"Yeah, but" is a built-in defense mechanism. It's not a completely bad thing, since in theory it can guide us to make informed choices as a result of serious questioning. However, it becomes a problem when we invest everything in our need to be right, the validity of our past experiences, what people have told us could happen, or what we're afraid might happen. Then it becomes limiting. If we go through life yeah butting, we can miss out on the new idea, the door opening, or the path to clarity.

To counter "Yeah, but," all we have to do is take a breath, allow the other person to share, and commit to listening honestly and openly. We may find we really don't agree with what we hear, but perhaps we can respond with "that's interesting" or "thanks for sharing," instead of "Yeah, but."

On the other hand, we may find we hear something amazing that changes our perspective or guides us toward what we've been envisioning. I find that such guidance often comes in the simplest forms.

Like when I'm at my computer struggling with what to write, and my daughter says, "Look at me, Mom. Look at me spin!" I so badly want to say, "Yeah, I see, but I'm busy. Yeah, that's great, but don't get hurt doing it." Instead, I stop what I'm doing, breathe, and watch the way she spins around in a circle. She's sharing with me in that moment, offering her wisdom.

*Mom, watch me spin, watch me live...look how free I am... look how I enjoy my moments...be like me...*I empty my cup. I see you, I hear you, I learn.

45

The truth about sticks and stones

WHEN KIDS SAY MEAN THINGS to each other, some do it to inflict harm, others out of immaturity or a lack of awareness.

Regardless of why things are said, it can be challenging to guide our children when they hear or say something mean. It's too easy to try to brush an incident off with a cliché such as "sticks and stones may break my bones, but words can never hurt me." Or we may toss out a response such as, "They're just words. Don't pay attention to what someone says."

The truth is, words are powerful.

Words are alive. They are the first step toward creating something, and they are what enable us to connect with someone. They are also how we form our guidelines for how we perceive and experience the world. This is why people who don't have the ability to speak or hear words use sign language to form them.

What a child hears on a day-to-day basis has a tendency to become what they believe. Not because the words are always true, but because they hear the words repeatedly. So to tell a child words don't mean anything is neither realistic nor honest. Words *do* mean something. When mean words are spoken, they can hurt. In contrast, when words are used lovingly, they can uplift and inspire.

Our choice of words in many ways defines who we are and who we want to be in the world. Do we want to tear people down, or do we want to raise them up? Do we want to do battle, or do we want to promote peace?

At the same time, words don't have to mean a thing. If someone calls you a name, you may feel the initial sting of it, but you then have a choice. Do you choose to accept the words as fact and make them part of your identity? Or would you prefer to release them, knowing they do nothing but weigh you down and disempower you?

Words that are intended to silence or disable us are poison and shouldn't be ingested. Whenever something is said with a negative intention, it's important to let it go, knowing that hate-filled words are a reflection of someone else's pain, someone else's inability to feel love—likely because of words they heard in their early years.

On the other hand, there are helpful and empowering words—words that make us feel good and inspire us to be kind, useful human beings. Beware of any temptation to reject such words when they are spoken about you, which we can tend to do because we're embarrassed. Don't let the things you need to believe about yourself cause you to feel sheepish.

The trick is to live in the paradox that words are both powerful and also mean nothing.

Instead of looking for a simple cut-and-dry response to give your kids, keep in mind that words and the communication skills they make possible require ongoing discussion. They invite a consistent dialogue about self-awareness, so that our children have a clear understanding of how they are taking the many things said to them.

In turn, our children will take responsibility both for the words they choose to use and the words they choose to believe.

46

Words are things, and these are the ones I love most

I ONCE HEARD MAYA ANGELOU say that words are things. She said that one day we will be able to measure the power of words, so we must be careful how we use them.

I believe this, mostly because I've always been very focused on words—sometimes to an extreme, as my husband will attest. Who knows why? I don't think this is uncommon, especially for writers.

Whatever the reason, I've long been cautious with words and conscious of their power to influence. Even as a little girl, I was preoccupied with words. They felt big to me, powerful. I noticed when words were unspoken. I also knew that once words were spoken, they were difficult to take back.

Maybe I was cautious to protect myself, to make sure I didn't get into trouble. Or maybe I was unsure of myself and didn't want to speak out of turn. Whatever the case, I knew for sure that I fully "felt" words when they were said or written.

Words can bring tears to my eyes, which I appreciate. But words can also cause me to wince, look away, or experience a headache. Some people claim that words "roll off their back."

For me, that's never been the case. So when Maya said "words are things," I couldn't agree more.

It's not just the word itself, but the intention behind the word. For instance, a swear word can be used to make a point or for humor. Swear words are great when they add definition or emotion to an experience. But when swear words are used to offend, oppress, or frighten, they take on a whole different meaning. Words are vehicles of expression. It's the intention behind the expression that causes them to have their "feel."

So what I have really been attracted to is the energy and feel of a word—or at least, how they feel to me, since each person has their own relationship with language, and each word has a different feeling depending on your own life story. Which is why my favorite words tend to change depending on what's going on in my life.

Right now, the following five words keep coming up for me. They are words that stabilize my sense of being:

1. Contentment. A state I aspire to, and therefore a word that evokes a sense of comfort and calm. Happiness feels like too much of a high—a high that can't be sustained—whereas contentment feels like a way of being, regardless of what's happening around me.

2. Humility. We need to take responsibility for our actions, yet nothing we do is done solely by ourselves. We need to make our own way in the world, although what this looks like is always the result of co-creation. We can enjoy life and be our best self—not so that we can be better than others, but so that we can make the world a better place. An aspect of humility involves embracing the paradox that while we are important, the world isn't about us. We are just one piece in a great big puzzle that somehow fits together. The universe has a natural perfection I certainly can't understand, let alone articulate, and yet I know it demands my heart-centered attention and faith. I know that we all play a role in something much grander than the mind can comprehend.

3. Bravery. Many believe bravery means you aren't afraid, whereas it means feeling afraid and moving forward anyway. I keep this in mind when I'm afraid, or when my children are afraid, because fear is completely normal. It's our response to fear that dictates the path of our lives. We can allow it to immobilize us, or it can propel us to a new sense of freedom.

4. Quiet. Since it's more socially acceptable to be extroverted than introverted, I wasn't always comfortable talking about my love of quiet. I love people, conversation, and group experiences, while at the same time, as I've already shared, I very much enjoy silence and being alone. This isn't easy for me, or for any other parent, since a parent's life is at times both busy and noisy 24/7. However, I've learned, often the hard way, that it's worth the energy to find time for quiet. Again, as I mentioned earlier, with doses of quiet throughout the day, I'm better able to connect with people, including my husband and children, in a way that feels authentic rather than forced.

5. Love. Perhaps we envision romance and partnership when we hear this word. But as we grow up, we realize it's much bigger. Love is our natural state of being and the thing that connects us. It's awareness of our light, as well as our ability to see the light in others, regardless of where any of us are on our journey. Love is a way of moving through the world, and a way of relating to other people. In any situation, we really only have two choices—love or fear. Although fear has become the norm in so many situations, we know it's love that feels right. Regardless of how corny it sounds, we all know deep down that love is always the right answer.

If I were to add a sixth word to my list of words, it would be gratitude. If we only noticed what's working in our lives, there's so much to be grateful for. I'm certainly grateful for words, because they outline my life—through writing, reading, teaching, and intimate conversations. They inspire me and lay the foundation for where I want to go next.

As Maya said, words are things. They are, without a doubt, the things that keep me connected.

COMMUNICATION

Cathy Cassani Adams, LCSW, CPC, CYT

47

The forced apology—a path to peace?

IT'S COMMON TO SEE parents forcing their children to apologize. Sometimes it results in the child saying "sorry." At other times it leads to increased conflict because the child refuses.

In the past, I too have asked my kids to say they were sorry, though for some reason I never felt good about it. Without real insight, an apology means nothing. It's just words, whose sole purpose is to pacify us. Words that create social comfort.

Was anything really learned? Does the child truly feel sorry, or are they just learning to use words to get out of an uncomfortable situation?

It's kind of like asking a child to lie. If they don't feel sorry, why force them to say it? Even worse, we punish them if they refuse to say sorry. What message are we sending them when we punish them for refusing to be false?

Instead of focusing on getting our children to apologize, how about we focus on the *feelings* involved? What was the feeling that brought on their behavior? Right before a child hit, yelled, or made a poor choice, what were they experiencing? If children can identify their feelings, they grow in self-awareness—and self-awareness leads to making better choices.

When one child does something to hurt another emotionally or physically, are both parties asked what happened? Do they each get an opportunity to explain their side? Maybe the situation isn't so cut and dry. Were there issues that led up to the present problem? A poor choice is rarely made in isolation. Instead of blaming, thereby creating a villain and a victim, can we see all sides of the situation?

By asking questions, both we and our children learn how one thing leads to another, and how seemingly little things can lead to big things. Even if only one child is at fault, at least that child gets an opportunity to share their perspective. This builds respect instead of causing shame. Validation replaces assumption. Children will integrate the lesson if they are first heard.

When children experience empathy, they learn how to be empathic. We want them to learn to really listen and understand the other person. Then, maybe the next time they feel anger, embarrassment, frustration, or some other emotion that upsets them, maybe they'll think before they speak or hit. They might try to take a deep breath, walk away from the situation, or ask for help.

Only when there's understanding can an apology be real. One or both parties will see the big picture, understand their role in the situation, and say, "I'm sorry."

Getting to this point may take longer than forcing an apology, and it may require more energy on our part. But it's how behavior changes. After all, what are we trying to teach when we demand an apology? How to make a mistake, say a few words, and walk away with no new understanding and no real remorse?

When such situations arise, as they inevitably will, the challenge is to focus on helping our children understand themselves and each other. In this way, we promote peace.

COMMUNICATION
Cathy Cassani Adams, LCSW, CPC, CYT

48

What are we teaching when we say, "I'm proud of you?"

SOMETIMES, WITH THE BEST of intentions, we send mixed messages to our children. We want them to think for themselves, be internally motivated, and not be overly influenced by other people's needs or opinions, yet the way we make them feel good is by telling them, "I'm proud of you."

There's obvious love and appreciation behind these words, nothing overtly harmful. But there's also an underlying message of what it means to feel worthy. The message is, "If you do something I or others approve of, then you'll feel good. If you do something that impresses me or others, you'll feel valued."

There's a measure of truth to this. It's great when parents notice gifts, talents, and hard work. But is this really how we would want to define success for our children? When they accomplish something, are we saying that their focus should be on the opinions of others, or their opinion of themselves?

Our task is to help our children feel comfortable on the inside, and to remind them that their most important influence needs to be their personal guidance system. Certainly we can support them by honoring what they do. But we also need to remind them to tap into how *they* feel about their accomplishments, because this is what will strengthen their inner compass.

Perhaps when our child brings home an A, instead of saying "I'm proud of you," we might say, "Wow, you must feel great about this!" It's a simple shift, but the message is completely different. Instead of them being happy because we praised them, we encourage them to feel their own joy, and we join in their celebration.

When children are young, many of us feel a need to constantly direct them or apply extensive external motivation in an attempt to influence their decision-making. But effective parenting is always aimed at helping them learn not to base their decisions on the approval of another, be it a peer or anybody else. The goal is that they should base their decisions on what feels right to *them*.

Then, as they move through life, they'll be guided by their own inner awareness instead of societal expectations. They'll place personal contentment above approval and popularity. They'll understand that while it's wonderful to have people notice their accomplishments, it's even better to feel aligned with their inner being and at peace with themselves.

I haven't given up saying "I'm proud of you." Sometimes these words describe perfectly how I'm feeling. But I try to balance such statements with phrases like, "What do you think about that?" or, "That must feel amazing!" My intention is always to hear about and witness their hard work, then hand back what's rightfully theirs.

49

Creating a respectful conversation with my daughter

JACEY AND I WERE ON a bike ride, with me in front and Jacey riding behind me, when the following conversation ensued.

Jacey: Mom, I want to ride alongside you on the sidewalk.

Me: I don't think there's enough room. I don't want us to hit each other. Come to think of it, you were riding side by side with your friend in front of the house today, and you were pretty close to hitting each other.

Jacey: There's enough room. We won't hit each other.

Me, nodding my head: Okay.

Jacey, as she rides up next to me: There's plenty of room, see.

Me: I do see, but I still don't feel comfortable with you there. I'm going to ride behind you. Go ahead in front of me.

Jacey: Okay, but there really is plenty of room. I can ride alongside my friends if I really want to.

Me, again nodding my head: All right.

One minute later, Jacey: Whoa, I just wobbled my wheel back and forth, and there isn't a lot of room on this sidewalk.

Mom: I agree.

Jacey: It's like super tight on the sidewalk!

Mom: Yes, it definitely feels tight.

Jacey: I fit on this sidewalk. But if there were two, it would be tight. If I ride next to someone, I could totally hit them if I fall over.

Mom: That's true.

Jacey: Now I'm going to beat you home.

This conversation required me to do a little breathing, and also watching. Not watching Jacey, but watching *myself.* You see, between each statement, I found myself experiencing emotions such as frustration, annoyance, irritation. This required me to create space between feeling the emotion and responding to my daughter. Without the space, I would have reacted.

It was like being in slow motion—a sort of moving meditation that gave me on-the-spot practice at being truly present. I wanted my daughter to listen to me; after all, I am the parent, right? I wanted her to agree with me and do what I suggested. I also needed her to "respect" me and not talk back.

Except that, that's not respect—it's control.

I could certainly offer a suggestion, but I couldn't force her to do it. I could share my feelings, but not compel her to agree. On the other hand, if I could share my viewpoint in a loving way and detach from how she received it, she might hear me.

Of course, to do this would require me to let go of needing to be "right." In other words, if I wanted her to hear me, I needed to hear *her.* If I wanted her to learn to listen to others, I needed to model real listening. This is something that isn't always easy, although it's always a choice.

Seen as a choice, it's wasn't about her—not about what she said or what she did. It was solely about me and my response.

COMMUNICATION

Cathy Cassani Adams, LCSW, CPC, CYT

The choice was to take what she was saying calmly, or to blow up because she wasn't listening to me and therefore wasn't showing me "respect."

Sometimes the space between the emotion I experience as a result of what my daughters say and the way I answer feels too small. I react in a way I don't like. But the wonderful thing is that I can always begin again, making a better choice next time. It takes practice.

Life has all kinds of ways of giving us lots of practice, even on a fun bike ride.

PRACTICE

Knowledge is of no value unless you put it into practice.

ANTON CHEKHOV

50

Change the world by practicing what you know

YOU BELIEVE IN SELF-AWARENESS, compassion, joy, love. You understand the importance of self-care, you adore reading books, and you love a great inspirational quote. You can also analyze yourself, even offer up observations to explain why you do what you do—though you keep doing the same thing, making the same choices, dealing with the same issues.

So, are you practicing what you know in everyday life, or is it just stuff you know in your head?

You read an inspiring book or article, feel like you "got" it, then proceed to tell others what you've learned. Or you have a life-altering experience, feel like you "got" it, then tell others why they should do what you do, what you did, or what you're going to do.

Except that there's no such thing as "got" it. There are no absolutes, no perfect plans. There's just moment-by-moment living, and within each of these moments we make choices.

A good choice is to notice your ego, your need to be right, your need to win, but instead of identifying with these "needs," step away from them.

PRACTICE

Cathy Cassani Adams, LCSW, CPC, CYT

You know it's important to be generous, but do you practice generosity in terms of your time, patience, love? You know it's helpful to meditate or engage in yoga, but do you take your meditation or yoga off the mat and practice balance in your everyday life? You know it's wise to love and forgive, but are you loving toward your husband when he's late or he forgets something? Do you forgive your children and your parents for their mistakes, or do you constantly remind them?

We cognitively know what feels good—what makes life uplifting. But too often we *think* it instead of *practice* it.

To practice something, we have to be conscious of our choices. If we live on autopilot, or move from thing to thing with no presence of being, it's hard to be loving, generous, compassionate. Living on autopilot recycles the same story, the same defensiveness, the same challenges—and the same outcomes.

Before you say, "I can't. That's too hard. I can't be expected to be conscious all the time," let go of "all the time" and just try *now*.

In other words, quit making a "plan" to be different and know there's no right time or perfect way. Let go of your most recent not-so-great choice, and choose differently *now*.

Equally as important, let go of the need to tell everybody else how to do things. While it's great to support one another, sharing stories, ideas, and suggestions, it's important to trust that others will find their way. They can't and shouldn't do it just like us, because they aren't us. Only we can be who we are, only we know what's best for us. The way to teach others is to practice being ourselves, which will inspire others to be themselves.

Whenever you think you've "got" it, remember that life isn't an academic or thought-based experience, but is experienced in real-time. A great quote, story, or book can direct you to a path of greater contentment, but it's practice in the moment that actually changes the world.

51

Practice saying no

MANY OF US HAVE IMPORTANT responsibilities that require our time. There are "musts" on our to-do list, essential and non-negotiable aspects of our daily experience that can't be skipped. I'm not unacquainted with the pressures of modern life.

Yet on many of our days, are there not activities that are optional, over which we might exercise some measure of choice?

Do you do what you *want* to do, or only what you think you *should* do? Do you volunteer at your kids' school because it makes you look like a great parent, or because it's a fun way of expressing yourself? Do you accept an invitation to a party because you'll enjoy being there, or because you hate to say no to the person who invited you or are afraid to miss out on being seen at such events?

Step back, take a breath, and notice what goes into your decision-making. It's wonderful to help others, but not if you are continually sacrificing yourself in the process. How can you authentically give of yourself if you are overwhelmed or depleted? How can you have fun at a social event if you really want to be at home relaxing?

Tuning into our desires takes practice. We have to step off

the treadmill for a time and actively listen for them. Only then can we make intelligent choices in those areas of our lives in which we have options, making decisions that truly serve us.

It takes letting go of being everything to everybody if we are to pay attention and really hear ourselves. If we don't, we're likely to end up resentful of those who ask for our time. But it isn't they who should be blamed for asking—it's our responsibility to answer them genuinely.

Today may be a good day to begin the practice of saying "no." No to things that don't feel good, and no to things that don't truly feel like *you*. This creates space for things that do feel right, such as an evening out with your partner, a long conversation with your child, or an afternoon nap.

Yes, a nap. You deserve it. How do I know this? Because we all do.

Instead of looking to the outside world for validation, why don't you validate yourself? Guilt may make an appearance, but just take a deep breath and let it pass right by you. Guilt is based on an old way of thinking and is an unnecessary self-depreciating form of martyrdom. Nobody can *make* you feel guilty. You choose to feel it. Which is why only you can let it go.

Now is the time to say no to unwanted obligations and yes to the things and individuals closest to your heart. Rather than focusing on people's perceptions of you, focus on how you feel on the inside.

This is your time, your life. Make the choices that honor who you are.

PRACTICE
Cathy Cassani Adams, LCSW, CPC, CYT

52

Give up the chaos and live in the moment

AFTER FIVE MONTHS OF construction and living in a rental, we moved back home. We had so much to unpack, but I was also anxious to get my Christmas stuff up. As if unloading boxes, unwrapping ornaments, and trying to catch up on three days' of unread email wasn't enough, my girls seemed to need something every few minutes—food, my attention, help.

I had my phone in my pocket, intending to make a quick call to my parents. But first I needed to unwrap one more ornament, put a pan away, finish my grocery list, and take the garbage bag out. In the midst of my flurry of activity, I started to laugh. I realized I was literally creating chaos.

I was *choosing* to be in chaos.

As the realization dawned on me that trying to do all these things simultaneously was to invite chaos, I began walking in circles for a while, mulling my choices.

It was then that I opted to ditch it all.

Since it was Sunday, Todd was home, and I decided to head to yoga class. After an hour of doing something for me, I returned home to my lists, computer, boxes, and holiday decorations. Everything not only looked different, but it felt different. I was ready to get going again, and this time had the girls help me instead of shooing them away so that I could do it *my* way. Doing it myself has always been my response to chaos.

I put my computer into hibernation, cautiously stepped around boxes, and focused on decorating my little tree. The difference now was that I felt connected to everything I was doing. This was always an option—I just hadn't taken it. Much of the time, we can choose what to do, how we feel, and how to respond to whatever may be happening around us.

Dropping everything and going to a yoga class isn't always possible, of course. But if yoga hadn't been an option, I could still choose to sit down and relax, take a breath, get a coffee, put on a good song, and in due course resume my tasks. In other words, I could bring an end to my self-created chaos by choosing not to participate in creating chaos.

Perhaps you feel there isn't a way you can stop—that you don't have choices. You feel you have to get *everything* done, and *you* have to do it all. But do you really? I know it may feel like it. I feel that way sometimes.

When I was single, in grad school, and working a job, I was crazy busy. Following this, Todd and I planned a wedding, and once again I was crazy busy. Then we had a baby. Oh, my goodness! Was I ever crazy busy now. So I had another baby, started a business, and had yet another baby. Do you see where I'm going with this? I was busy in all of those situations, and I'm still busy to this day. When does it end? When do I finally get to enjoy my everyday life?

I think now is a good time.

When it comes to my everyday life, there's never a place and time when everything's done, everything's neat and tidy. Every day, there's something more to do. When today's list is

PRACTICE

Cathy Cassani Adams, LCSW, CPC, CYT

done, there'll be a new list tomorrow.

Can you let go of some things you don't want to do and know it's okay? Can you say "no" and disappoint someone, yet know you're still a good person? Can you go to bed without completing every task, but feel fulfilled and sleep peacefully anyway?

It's important to realize that life isn't something that's being *done to* us, and that we are always free to choose, which is what freewill means.

If big things are happening around you, you may well feel worried, if not afraid. This is all the more reason to love yourself, soothe yourself, and choose to engage in activities that make you feel good. By fortifying yourself in this way, you equip yourself to handle the things you can't control. In fact, when you take care of yourself first, you'll be amazed how good you will feel—and, ironically, how much you will accomplish.

Of course, there is always the option of deciding you can't do what I'm suggesting. If this is truly the case, at least enjoy the chaos! After all, some people love chaos. They relish having loads of things on their to-do list. Feeling overwhelmed, overworked, or maybe just needed is important to their sense of identity. If this is true of you, then acknowledge it. It will not only help you understand yourself better, but it will keep you from blaming others for your busy schedule.

Life is just a series of moments, one moment following the next, creating the story of your life. What will your next moment be like? It's yours to choose.

53

Listen, be there, or let go

SKYLAR HAD TO GO BACK to the dentist for the second time in less than a week and wasn't too excited about it. The evening before, I explained what the dentist would do and why. When she asked if I would be with her and hold her hand, I assured her I would.

When we arrived for the appointment, I was told I couldn't go in with her. Their policy was for parents to remain in the waiting room. "I understand the policy," I said, "but I already told my daughter I would stay with her."

The hygienist explained that kids are calmer when the parents aren't present. "I'm sure that in many situations, you're right," I agreed. "However, I told my daughter I would hold her hand."

The hygienist said I could walk back with her, although the dentist would probably ask me to leave. I nodded, and we walked back to the surgery, where I quietly sat on the floor and placed my hand on Skylar's stomach. Neither speaking nor moving, I remained there while the team prepared to fill her cavity. The dentist walked in, we smiled at each other, and he sat down and started working. I stayed on the floor, out of view. Crying a little, Skylar occasionally grabbed my hand.

This wasn't my first "floor" experience. I had been here many times before with my other daughters, sitting in a gymnastics class with one of them, a kindergarten room with another. I was also experienced in being the only adult wading around a "child only" class, as well as the only parent who stays for the birthday party.

Now they are older. They walk into a new classroom unassisted, ride their bikes to practice by themselves, head into a dentist or doctor appointment with confidence, go up to their room with their friends, and politely let me know they don't need me around. Once they were scared, but now they aren't, which could be from growing up and becoming more mature. But part of it also came from having their hand held, having someone there for them. Because they experienced what it is to feel secure, they integrated a sense of security.

Twenty minutes later, the dentist and hygienist had finished their work. Looking up at both of them from the floor, I thanked them for listening to me and accommodating my daughter's needs.

It hasn't always been clear to me when I should stay and when I should go, and I recognize that I have to strike a balance. I have never found such occasions easy to deal with. My best answer in such situations is to listen. I try to hear my children when they say they're scared, trust them when they say they need support, and most importantly show up when I say I'll be there.

When we arrived home from the appointment, Skylar was feeling good and wanted to play with her neighborhood friend. I asked if she wanted me to walk with her. She responded, "No, I'll go by myself." I listened, then watched her walk down the street.

54

Sleeplessness, anxiety, and a sick child

My plan was to go to bed extra early, but I found myself climbing into bed around 10:30, much later than I had anticipated. At least I was packed and ready to go away with my husband in the morning. Getting away for a long weekend as a couple isn't easy, which is why we hadn't done this for five years.

Then, just as I was settling in, I heard a crying child—a sound I didn't hear much nowadays since our girls were nine, seven, and four. As I walked down the hall to my youngest daughter's bedroom, I recognized the cry. Even before I touched her, I knew she was hot. So I put her in bed with me, hoping it was because she'd been in the sun all day. Then I found myself awake the rest of the night going over possible scenarios of "what ifs."

When my husband got up at 5 a.m. to fly out earlier than me so he could get some work done before I arrived, I was still awake. As he left, I told him I'd see him soon, though in the back of my mind I really wondered if this would be the case. Knowing I wasn't going to get any sleep, I got up. Realizing I needed my morning clear to take Skylar to the doctor, I made the decision to let my college students know I wouldn't be teaching the morning class. At least this brought me some peace of mind. Around 7:30 a.m., my mother-in-law (GG) arrived because she was going to watch the girls while we were away. I left for the doctor, and she helped my other two get ready for school.

Within ten minutes of arriving at immediate care, I learned it was strep throat. My daughter rarely gets sick and had never been on antibiotics, but today was the day. Dropping her off at home with GG, I headed to Walgreens for a prescription. As I drove, I was so tired and so bummed, I started to cry.

Pulling myself together as I entered the pharmacy, I sat down to wait for the medicine. It was an opportunity to call my husband to discuss our options. As my crying resumed, I ran through the possibilities with him. Maybe I shouldn't go at all. Or maybe I could show up tomorrow. Maybe he could fly back home and we could have a fun weekend in the city.

My husband lovingly disagreed with my suggestions, assuring me his mom could take care of Sky and that everything would be fine. Nevertheless, I continued to cry because I felt I had to make the decision. Without sleep, and anxious just because I was a mom, this caused me to cry louder, so that the elderly people waiting for their prescriptions began looking at me, concerned.

It was then that I remembered to breathe. Even with sleep deprivation, I knew I had whipped myself into a frenzy and needed to breathe. As I did so, I let go of telling myself negative stories and released my fear, anxiety, and sleeplessness.

In that momentary peace, I thought about using the coin toss. Not for the coin to tell me what to do, but to figure out how I really felt. If I was excited about the outcome, I would know it was right. If the toss bummed me out, I would know what I really wanted.

Instead of using a coin, I thought about what I wanted to

hear GG say when I arrived home. What would feel better—that she wanted me to go, or that she wanted me to stay? Visualizing both scenarios, I allowed myself to feel how happy it would make me to hear her say, "Go." So I knew what I wanted to do. And when I actually got home, GG told me right away that she was completely comfortable staying with Skylar, and that if I felt comfortable going, I should go.

The big test still lay ahead of me. When I went up to Skylar's room to administer her medication, she slowly took it, her eyes closed, then she lay back down with her back to me. Thinking she was soothed by my presence, I remained seated on the floor next to her bed—until she slowly turned around, looked at me, and said, "You can go now."

Although I knew she meant I should leave the room so that she could sleep, somehow I felt she was offering me the gift of approval. Whereupon my sister-in-law called and also told me to go, which was followed by a text from my friend saying to have fun, and a text from my parents telling me to have a good time. Finally, my older girls arrived home for lunch and assured me they would be fine—that they were excited about their time with GG, and that they would help take care of Skylar. To top it all off, I received a text from my husband, a hopeful message reminding me to take care of myself and trust that all would be fine.

So I found myself in a taxi on the way to the airport, and then on a plane. Though every thirty minutes or so I cried a little because I was feeling uncomfortable and sad, I was nevertheless happy with my choice. I was sitting in a middle seat, so the guy to my left kept his earphones on, ignoring me, while the woman to my right kept offering me gum.

To restore a sense of balance, I pulled out my notebook

PRACTICE
Cathy Cassani Adams, LCSW, CPC, CYT

and began writing from stream-of-consciousness. Almost immediately, I saw the words that always bring me back to reality: *What are you going to choose, love or fear?* They are my life mantra, though even they can be forgotten in a state of sleeplessness and anxiety.

The thoughts that ran through my head followed two different tracks. Do I move forward in fear of what could happen? Sky could get sicker, the older girls could get sick, maybe GG gets sick. What if I get sick? What if I feel sad the whole trip? Or do I move forward with love? After all, everyone was supporting me as I took this trip, my husband was waiting for me, all was well, good things awaited, so I should trust the process and enjoy the adventure.

I knew which one felt better, and I knew who I wanted to be in this situation.

The tears stopped and I stepped off the plane to find my husband waiting with roses, excited I was joining him in Arizona to celebrate our ten-year anniversary. Before I could say anything, he handed me his phone so that I could listen to a voice message from GG: "Sky woke up and her fever is gone. She's downstairs watching television, doing great."

I breathed.

55

Time for a hug

Every day, I make a point to hug each member of my family. Not just a quick hello or goodbye hug, but a longer out of-the-blue kind of hug. Sometimes I hear, "Oh, Mom," or see an eye-roll, but they let me hug, and they hug back.

While hugging, I say nothing. I'm just quiet, and I breathe. I let go of what happened before, or what comes next, and simply hug. After a minute or two we move on, back to our busy day, going here and there. But for those moments, I'm there, fully aware. These hugs have become a way of practicing mindfulness—a way to appreciate a few minutes of peace and stability.

It's hard for me to believe how fast my daughters are growing. It's even harder for me to believe they once weighed only about seven pounds and were completely dependent on me. But that's the cycle. We move into and out of different ages, growing, changing. We feel like time is moving fast.

That's why hugging is so important. It's an opportunity to be present, conscious of what's happening right now. It's a way to connect with my husband and girls, embracing who they are at that moment. I also find I reconnect with myself, as I notice that I'm on autopilot, lost in my to-dos, or worrying about

PRACTICE
Cathy Cassani Adams, LCSW, CPC, CYT

181

things that don't really matter. It's a way to increase my self-awareness, an opportunity to notice where I'm putting my energy.

It feels good to check things off my list and plan what needs to get done tomorrow. But I also want to be present today. Hugging reminds me to slow down and *be here,* so that I don't have to wonder where the time went. It helps me stay connected on a daily basis, instead of having to try to reconnect in a time of crisis.

Life can trick us into thinking we're too stressed or too busy. We can get caught up in thinking that work or cleaning the house is so very important. But at some level, don't we all know what's most important? Which is why we need to practice paying attention, even when we have busy schedules and pressing responsibilities—even when we're worried about what happened yesterday or what could happen tomorrow.

The only time we can do *anything* is *right now.* And right now, there's plenty of time and nothing more important than a long and quiet hug.

56

Let go of the "role" and just be you

Several years ago, while frantically putting our girls to bed, my husband asked why I was rushing. Without thinking, I responded, "I just want them to go to sleep so that I can be me again."

I heard my words, and I was taken aback. All night I thought about what I had said and what it meant.

Was I not myself when I was with my children?

I realized that much of the time, I wasn't. Somewhere along the way, I had taken on the *role of mom,* a role characterized by seriousness, worry, multitasking, and martyrdom. Typical maybe, but it didn't suit me. I felt drained, disconnected, and more than ready to be done at the end of the day.

My children never asked me to take on this role, I just adopted it. Instead of integrating my mom skills into my existing self, I split myself and became a different person depending on what I was doing. And like many moms, I began losing my identity, my sense of being, and my ability to relate to my family in a way that was authentic.

Roles can get complicated, whereas I like to keep it simple. I prefer to trust my gut, use common sense, and just be "me."

PRACTICE

Cathy Cassani Adams, LCSW, CPC, CYT

This means dancing in the kitchen, singing in the car, spending time with my friends, making mistakes, talking about my feelings, crying when I'm sad—and most important, laughing a lot. Some days are wonderful, and I make sure to acknowledge joyful moments. Other days are difficult, and part of my parenting job is to model how to handle challenges, take responsibility, and accept situations for what they are.

More and more, rather than putting all of my energy into a role, I put my energy into being myself. I wake up and *show up* so that my kids can know their mom. I want them to see me fall down, get back up, experience success, handle rejection, and have fun.

Instead of needing it to be bedtime, I'd rather enjoy the days. In preference to striving for kudos from others, I'd rather strive to be the best version of myself, with the hope that my girls choose to do the same.

LIVING WHAT YOU WANT YOUR KIDS TO LEARN
Cathy Cassani Adams, LCSW, CPC, CYT

57

How to move on after a mistake

WHEN SOMEONE ELSE MAKES a mistake, we often understand. But when it comes to ourselves, we tend to have difficulty forgiving ourselves.

I used to deny my mistakes, and sometimes I blamed others. At other times, I sat in my mistakes for days, just to punish myself.

None of that worked very well. It just made everything worse.

One day, I was late picking up my daughter—late enough that she had to go to the office. It was a big mistake, the result of not watching the time. I was the only one to blame, so I was forced to feel it. I find that's the hardest part—feeling it. I had to sit with my daughter and let her cry, holding her as she released all those feelings of being forgotten, even if it was only for ten minutes. She was right to feel the way she did. I would feel the same. It was appropriate that I sit with her, quietly experiencing the discomfort of being wrong.

I know there are worse experiences in the world. After all, she was safe at school and with people she knew. It ended up fine.

PRACTICE
Cathy Cassani Adams, LCSW, CPC, CYT

185

But that's where we go wrong. We compare pain. We justify or disregard someone's pain because it could have been worse.

In that moment, what my daughter needed was to be heard, not told why she shouldn't be feeling what she was feeling. So I let her feel it. I didn't offer an excuse. I just said, "Yes, this happened, and it was my fault. I'm so sorry. I love you."

When she eventually fell asleep following lots of questions, talking, and apologies, I sat on the stairs and cried. I worried about trusting myself. I worried that if this happened, what else might I forget? I thought about all the notes on my desk, all the emails that needed a response, all the commitments I'd made, all the events on my calendar. And I just felt it all—all my imperfections, my fears, my shame. I also shared it with my husband.

I walk a tightrope most days, trying to balance everything, hold everyone up, keep it together. I consider myself an excellent tightrope walker. Most of us moms are up there every day. But every once in a while, I fall, and it hurts.

After the crying and sharing, I drank some water. I walked around, picked some things up off the floor, and started to ease back into the flow of the day. When my daughter woke up, she wanted to sit on my lap. Saying she felt better, she wanted to hug for a long time. Then she told me stories about her day and did a few dances while she talked.

I listened, and realized I was better, too. We were better because we felt it. We sat in the pain of the moment and felt it. It may be small in hindsight, but it felt big when it showed up, and we both felt it. Then it was over. We were done with it because we dealt with it.

I have worked through so much past pain—pain that I stifled. I learned that to feel better, I have to acknowledge the pain.

LIVING WHAT YOU WANT YOUR KIDS TO LEARN

Cathy Cassani Adams, LCSW, CPC, CYT

Maybe not all at once, but at least to realize it's there. Because if I refuse to look at it, it will show up in different ways—in insecurity, poor choices, lying, hiding, or physical pain.

If you made a mistake today, or yesterday, or a long time ago, consider looking at it again. Consider taking responsibility if necessary, apologizing sincerely. Don't blame anyone else. Just acknowledge, feel it, speak it, and watch it disappear.

This is one of the ways we practice self-respect, and this is how we teach self-respect.

PRACTICE
Cathy Cassani Adams, LCSW, CPC, CYT

58

Want to stay calm when your child gets angry?

HOW CAN WE HELP OUR children when they are angry, frustrated, disappointed, or sad?

The key is to start by staying calm. We don't need to argue, defend, or join them in their emotional upheaval. Instead, it's important we just breathe, relax, and stay grounded.

It's not easy, I know.

Feeling frustrated or angry with our children is often the reaction we have when we're on autopilot. Accessing our inner calm takes awareness and practice. We need to create the space to choose a more helpful response. How can we do this?

Call it whatever you want—meditation, quiet time, nothingness, breathing, relaxation, sitting in stillness. It isn't the term that matters, but actually taking the time to practice what the term points to.

You don't have to take a class or buy a bunch of books before you can practice becoming quiet. Not that I'm against either classes or books. It's just that they aren't essential. I've studied many different types of formal meditation, and I know many who swear by a certain teacher or practice. But for me, trying to follow specific guidelines turned out to be a distraction.

Now, I simply take some time in the mornings, anywhere from five to fifteen minutes, to sit, breathe, and relax. At one time this was a task on my to-do list, whereas over time it became something I enjoy and look forward to doing. I sit comfortably and surround myself with things I love, such as pictures, quotes, candles, gifts from my kids, rocks I picked up on the beach. Then I close my eyes and breathe.

Sometimes the day starts off crazy and I forget all about quiet time. But let me tell you, I can tell the difference. I'm more distracted throughout the day, more easily agitated, more readily offended, and more frequently annoyed by little things.

Accessing a calm state isn't only valuable in terms of parenting skills. It's beneficial for our overall health. It can improve sleep and heighten immunity. It increases our sense of wellbeing. And it helps us quiet our continuous thoughts. In fact, that's really the best part of entering into quietness—it helps us distance ourselves from our incessant and often unhelpful thoughts, leaving us feeling more centered and clear.

It takes a little practice to get used to sitting with yourself, but you can start simply. Sitting in the car waiting for your children, close your eyes and deep breathe for a minute or two. Or before you start work at your computer, breathe deeply for a full minute. As you begin to notice the benefits, you can incorporate stillness into other parts of your day.

Practicing a few minutes or more a day will increase the likelihood you'll stay calm in the most difficult moments. Not only will you feel better about the way you respond to challenges, but you'll teach your children the importance of accessing their own inner stillness. They'll learn from your example that calmness begins inside, regardless of what's happening in their outside world.

PRACTICE
Cathy Cassani Adams, LCSW, CPC, CYT

59

Five-minute meditation for busy parents

YOU'RE IN A HURRY. Perhaps you don't even have to be anywhere, but you're acting as if you're trying to get somewhere. After all, if you're like most people, you've been *trained* to be in a hurry, to move fast, to get a lot done in the least amount of time.

So why do you have the feeling you don't know what happened between waking up and going to bed, except that you moved fast and felt extremely busy? Why does it feel like time is passing you by and the kids are growing up so fast?

The reality is that many of us are disconnected from our day. We go through the motions of living life, but we're not "here." Life feels like it's zipping past us because our mind is always somewhere else, trying to take care of something else.

How to rectify this?

The answer is to make a decision to be *present* in the present.

If you want to be here, you have to practice being here. To illustrate, do something simple like walking somewhere, anywhere, with your children. Don't just walk with them, but walk at their pace. Don't pull them along or tell them to hurry up. Allow them to lead. Watch them as they enjoy looking around.

See how they observe the world, stop to pick things up, or use the curb as a balance beam. They are in the moment, moving in response to their feelings.

You'll likely hear your mind telling you, "This is silly. You're wasting time. What's the point of this?" When this happens, just notice your need to rush, move quickly, not be present. Notice it and question it. Realize it's a programmed response that keeps you on autopilot all day long. As you notice, remember to breathe. Breathe in and out deliberately, calming your mind and relaxing your central nervous system.

If you do this, when your children grab your hand, you'll actually *feel* them grabbing your hand. Then you can focus your full attention on their hand. Notice the way it feels and the way it looks. But avoid the temptation to create a story around the feel of their hand, telling yourself it should or shouldn't feel a certain way. Just feel what *is*.

As you walk, smell the air, hear the birds, and see the trees. Look at your children and take note of their faces, their hair, their age. Look into their eyes and smile, allowing them to really *feel* your smile.

They will remember you in that moment, and you will remember them.

All you have to do is practice this every day for five minutes. In those five minutes, time will slow down. You will feel peaceful. You will know your children, and they will know you.

PRACTICE

Cathy Cassani Adams, LCSW, CPC, CYT

NOTICE

Be content in with what you have, rejoice in the way things are.
When you realize nothing is lacking,
the whole world belongs to you.

LAO TZU

Today, I noticed

MY DAUGHTER HAS PLAYED soccer for three or more years now. I've gone to the games, cheered, and generally done the things moms do. She has always enjoyed playing and was looking forward to the season. However, for me the games have blended into one another—just a lot of kicking, running, and snacks.

But today, at her first game of the season, I found myself sitting bolt upright and staring. She was playing as usual, but she was a different person. Her body was moving fluidly, she kept her eye on the ball, and she was assertive when she kicked. She had changed.

The game was typical in that she had some assists and some awesome defense, to the point that I found myself yelling "good job" a lot. Though she didn't score any goals or experience any moments of glory, she didn't need them. She just looked like an athlete, a real member of the team.

Much of the game, I felt I could cry as I watched her move with grace, express confidence, and demonstrate that she knows more about this sport than I will ever know. She was truly competing in today's game. I don't know whether this was just for today, or for the season, or for many years to come. It doesn't really matter.

What matters is that today, I noticed.

61

She chose great, and so do I

A WHILE BACK—I honestly can't remember when—I decided to respond to the question, "How are you today?" with the answer, "Great!" Or if not great, maybe wonderful or something along those lines. The exact word isn't something I even think about anymore, it's become such a habit.

You may ask, "Is this always true?"

Here's how I look at it. Even if something isn't so wonderful, or something is scary, or I'm feeling stressed, there are still a lot of things that are great. My response to people may not reflect everything in my day or every aspect of my being, but it's an answer that defines a daily choice to notice that a lot of things are indeed great.

Every single day we have a choice. Some days I wake up and notice what I'm not getting, what I'm afraid of, what I've lost, or why things aren't fair. But I've learned over and over again that this doesn't help, doesn't do anything to make my day better. It only makes my day heavy and empty, and I blame everyone around me for the thoughts that go round and round in my head.

Whenever I choose to notice my fears, insecurities, or issues—because they *are* there, and maybe even need to be addressed—I simultaneously notice the big tree in the front yard, my really good coffee, my favorite flip flops, and my sleeping family. In other words, I realize that a lot of things are great.

When I drove my daughter Camryn to camp, which was a big deal for her (and me) since she would be staying a few nights, a counselor greeted her and then asked her a series of questions. The questions mostly dealt with health, such as, "Have you been in contact with a sick person, do you take medication, do you have an inhaler?" But the last question was, "How are you feeling right now?"

"Great!" she said.

I smiled for many reasons—not least of which were that I think she hears her mom say this a lot, and that the counselor responded, "That's the first *great* I've heard all day."

What she taught me in that moment was that when we say "great," we not only affect the way we're feeling, but we affect the people who hear us. The counselor not only broke out into a huge smile when she heard my daughter's response, but she wrote *GREAT!!!* in all caps with extra exclamation marks on my daughter's check-in sheet.

Another reason it made me smile was that I realized Camryn made a choice. She was super-nervous and really worried about the camp experience. Simultaneously, she was excited.

So she made a choice. She chose *"Great."*

62

What are you sharing today?

DOES IT FEEL EASIER to be negative sometimes? Or maybe more normal? It certainly seems more socially acceptable to share our problems rather than our joys. Perhaps it feels more comfortable to talk about difficulties rather than awesomeness. Maybe it helps us fit in.

Or is it just a habit?

I don't mean to say it isn't helpful to talk about our challenges with those we trust. For me, it's a regular practice. I find it a necessary part of emotional wellness, a way to release what I don't need. But when negativity is our go-to conversation, and when we only share what's difficult, it seems to dull the atmosphere. It certainly dulls the senses.

What if we normalized sharing the good, too? Not in a bragging, inauthentic, "I'm better than you" kind of way, but in an "I'm feeling very thankful, thank you for asking" way.

Rather than causing us to feel somehow less than another, we could allow the good things happening in their life to inspire us, realizing that in the big picture shared feelings of wellness benefit us all.

The other day I ordered coffee. The woman who rang me

up said, "You're just a little too chipper today, aren't you?"

I pondered her question. Yes, I could dull-out and tell her how things are hard, that I have a headache, or that I'm running behind—all the things that go into a typical conversation. In fact, as I talked about earlier, I have an inner seventh-grade self that would prefer to do this. She's on high alert when someone appears annoyed, since she worries she won't be liked or might be misunderstood. She learned to protect herself by focusing on things that suck. It's how she found a way to fit in, stay safe.

Except that I'm not twelve anymore, and all of my challenges in life have taught me one thing: *I'm grateful to be here.*

I don't have a perfect life—nobody does. But I know that every moment can feel pretty good when I'm present for it. And if a moment doesn't feel good, I know it's mine to work on or mine to view in a different way. What I feel in each moment is always my decision.

I answered the lady who served me coffee by saying, "I just feel really good right now." And she smiled.

63

A ten-year-old sees the beauty in the simple

MY DAUGHTER WAS OUTSIDE collecting bits of glass from the street. I resisted the urge to ask why, or to tell her she should be careful. She was turning ten that month, so I had begun the process of gently letting go and trusting.

She came inside with a bag of different-colored pieces of glass, marveling at what she had found. Beauty in the simple things, I thought. We cleaned out an old glass jar that was once filled with olives, and she placed her tiny treasures in it.

It's so simple to find beauty in the everyday and the ordinary. To notice what's working, even when it seems broken. To love something that may seem unnecessary or discarded, when really it just hasn't found its place yet—hasn't found where its beauty will be recognized.

My daughter plans to find more glass to fill up the jar. She's excited about her new discovery.

To me, her findings are remarkable, a lovely view of something that has always been there.

64

Trusting our kids as they cross the street

EVERY DAY WHEN I DROP OFF my kids at school, I stop at a crosswalk as a guard assists children across the street. Most days, to my joy, I get to see a fifth-grader named Max cross the street by himself. He high-fives the crossing guard, and some days he even gives her a big hug right there in the middle of the street.

Max, who's the same age as my oldest daughter, has Down Syndrome. I've met his parents, though I don't know them well; I appreciate watching them interact with him in the mornings. His dad gives him a kiss and hug before Max ventures off to the crosswalk. Then dad watches until Max is safely in school. If Max turns around, his dad always smiles and waves. Even more importantly, his dad exudes a confidence—an inner certainty— that I'm sure Max picks up on. Of course, I would never assume to know what either of them is thinking; but as I watch, the word I *feel* is "trust."

The whole process of Max getting to school *exudes* trust. It says, "I trust who you are, I trust in what you can do, and you can trust me to be here if you need me." My morning encounters with Max remind me how important it is to reflect this for my own children.

Instead of carrying anxiety about what my kids can or can't do, will or won't do, I would much rather stand back, watch, love, and trust.

I once heard life coach Martha Beck say, "If you are scared, then you are scary. If you are calm, then you are calming." I don't want to be scary. I don't want to contribute to whatever fear or anxiety my girls may already carry. I want to be a supportive daily presence, a calm in their busy and sometimes hectic lives.

I'm human and emotional, so I won't do this perfectly. But it's an important awareness for me, an important self-observation. I want my children to live their own lives and trust they can handle whatever comes their way—something that's a lot easier if they know I trust them and believe in what they can do.

NOTICE
Cathy Cassani Adams, LCSW, CPC, CYT

65

How to have a relationship with your children as they grow

I WAS CROSSING THE STREET with my ten-year-old daughter and reached out to hold her hand. She didn't pull away, but I saw her smile. It was her way of saying, "Mom, I don't need you to do this anymore." I love holding my daughter's hand, but I recognize she no longer requires my guidance to cross the street. She's entering pre-adolescence, which means she has the ability and responsibility to handle many things without me.

Though this transition can be challenging, it's also exhilarating. It's such a joy to watch my daughter grow, to have more meaningful conversations with her, to broaden our relationship.

As parents, we need to honor our children's development and shift with it. If we are to make our relationship with our kids our priority, we too have to grow continually. We have to grow out of the need to do everything for them, letting go of what was, so that what's supposed to come next can naturally and organically unfold.

Often we hold on too tightly, imagining the connection can remain the same. But love is about letting go. It's about creating space so that our children can expand. If we hold them to an outdated version of our relationship with them, they become inauthentic, grow quietly resentful, or rebel.

I think of a three-year-old who looks me in the eye and says, "No, I do it myself!" It's easy to take offense when our kids begin to be independent. Instead, we need to see this change as their way of signaling that our relationship with them needs to evolve. They are asking for greater freedom.

Keeping my daughter safe will always be my priority. However, what I consider "safe" needs continual redefinition. Instead of holding her hand as we cross the street, I now need to stay interested in what she has to say, ask the important questions, and listen intently and respectfully regardless of her answers. I need to be present so that she knows I'm accessible.

I need to be willing to trust my daughter's choices so that she learns to trust herself. I need to be mature enough to allow her to drop my hand when her friends are around, then grab it again, no questions asked, when she's feeling alone or afraid. It is my job to be open, allowing her to take the lead. It's about letting her tell me through her words or actions that she needs a little more room to become who she's meant to be.

NOTICE

Cathy Cassani Adams, LCSW, CPC, CYT

66

"I guess I'll work it out"

CAMRYN WAS GETTING READY for a play date with a lot of girls. She was excited, but she was also a little leery. I sat and listened as she shared her concerns—issues such as how one girl always wants to take care of a certain girl, and how this girl doesn't really know this girl. "What will you do in these situations?" I asked.

To my surprise, she smiled really big and said, "I guess I'll work it out."

It was clear she needed nothing from me. No words, no encouragement. As I continued to look at her, processing what she had said, it occurred to me how simple it all was, largely because she was so trusting. With this simple statement, she reminded me how worry is so unnecessary, and how fear achieves nothing except to generate more fear.

I thought about how, for over forty years, I have "worked it out," regardless of the situation in which I found myself. So why do I often find myself dwelling on my concerns and mistrust my ability to deal with whatever a day sends my way?

Life can only be dealt with one moment at a time, as situations actually arise. It isn't possible to deal with the worries I have about what might happen, and all the scenarios I paint in my head, because none of them are real. I can only make decisions that need to be made from moment to moment. Like Camryn, I can share my concerns and process my emotions, but in the end I really have to trust and appreciate that things will work out.

What relief I felt in that moment. In fact, it was a tremendous relief to realize I don't need to plan it all, work it out in my mind in advance, or create a solution to every mentally-generated problem. Instead, I can let go and just be present in this moment now, trusting I'll be the "me" I've always been and make the best possible choices when the need arises.

And if I don't make the best choice? Then I trust my ability to make adjustments, say I'm sorry, or find another way—like so many times before. This is the way a child thinks and responds. Yet it's not a childish way of thinking. It's what faith is really about.

The challenge is to retain awareness of this, keeping what it feels to be this free at the forefront of our thinking. Will I forget? Of course. Probably over and over again. But like so many times before, I know I'll work it out.

67

Are your kids really ungrateful?

YOU COOK A GREAT MEAL, plan a terrific party, or change your work schedule to volunteer at school. But somehow your children seem ungrateful. Not only do they seem ungrateful, but they actually complain about the experience, wishing it were better or different.

I know this is infuriating. I've felt the sting of unrecognized parenting efforts many times.

But that's just it. Our kids are often challenged to recognize what they don't understand. How can they be expected to grasp the logistics of a big meal or party, or relate to leaving work early? They can't begin to understand the daily challenges of an adult—which is a good thing, if you think about it. They are children and need to live in a child's world.

As much as we would like our children to validate and admire our efforts, this doesn't often happen. Not because they are ungrateful or unkind, but because they are still learning to see beyond their own experiences. As parents, we tend to view their lives through an adult lens, expecting them to understand life the way we do. But to offer reasoned and consistently polite responses is an adult skill that our children are only just learning.

They are still developing their insight and hindsight.

The things we interpret as ingratitude are actually fantastic teaching opportunities. What better way to teach compassion and the importance of noticing the good than with a real-life example? Instead of being offended by our children, or shaming them for not understanding the bigger picture, we can make it a point to discuss what they may not have noticed.

Naturally, I'm occasionally triggered by a less-than-grateful response or unappreciative complaint. I've dealt out my share of what-about-me reactions. But when the dust settles, it always becomes obvious that my kids just want what I want. They long to be heard and validated, which means being free to share what they are feeling.

Often a comment about a party being bad isn't about the party at all. It's about what someone said or did at the party. Similarly, a negative attitude at dinner may not be about the food that was cooked, but is just the releasing of accumulated stress from school.

Instead of deciding that our kids are ungrateful, maybe we can first ask questions and do our best to view the situation from their perspective.

68

Teaching children to thank the Earth

MY GIRLS AND I HAD BEEN in the car a long time. When we pulled up at our final destination, they all said they were car sick. Nobody moved, and my youngest looked like she was about to cry.

Since we were parked in front of my sister's house, I told everyone to get out and lie on the grass. When they just sat there, continuing to complain, I walked over to the grass, lay on my back, and said, "I mean it. Lie down next to me."

They lay flat on their backs. Whereupon I told them to spread their arms and legs wide and close their eyes. Then I invited them to let go of whatever didn't feel good, allowing the earth to take it. "The earth will always support you," I explained. "It's always here, holding us up, and it's always willing to absorb, cleanse, and offer us whatever we need to survive." I instructed them to breathe deeply, feel the sun on their faces, notice the wind, and relax into the ground.

We were quiet for at least three minutes. Then my oldest said she felt better. When she got up, her sisters followed. My youngest said, "Thanks, Mom!"

I said, "Don't thank me, thank the earth."

LIVING WHAT YOU WANT YOUR KIDS TO LEARN
Cathy Cassani Adams, LCSW, CPC, CYT

As they ran to my sister's door, they laughed and yelled, "Thanks, earth!"

I stayed an extra minute, realizing we don't teach kids to love the earth with just words. We need to remind them how to reconnect, to remember what it provides, and to be in awe of its power. Oneness and connectedness can't be learned through a book but have to be felt in the body. We need to feel how it all fits together—how everything has a natural order, and how if we fail to care for what sustains us, we will no longer be sustained.

I opened my eyes and looked at the tree above me, aware of how it provides us with clean air. I felt the ground beneath me holding me up. I saw a group of birds flying in unison, cooperating with each other because they know their survival depends on such cooperation. I was reminded to notice and feel so that I can teach my children to notice and feel.

Then someone drove by and honked at the lady lying on the ground. I laughed, realizing it was my cue to get up. Just like my girls, I got up and returned to the day in a better state.

NOTICE
Cathy Cassani Adams, LCSW, CPC, CYT

Believing in Santa

WHEN I WAS EIGHT OR NINE years old, I remember lying in bed on Christmas Eve thinking about Santa. The funny thing was, I wasn't really envisioning gifts or the way he would get into my house. I was just feeling good. Everything seemed magical.

I always think about that when I think of Santa. Of course, I loved Santa's presents, but that's not really what Santa gave me. Santa made me feel like everything was right in the world, things were on track, and at least for Christmas Eve I could forget about being anxious or concerned about situations and just fall into the goodness of it all.

That's why I believe in Santa. He's a symbol of goodness and fairness, and he reminds me of what I fail to notice a lot of the time. Though he happens to pop up in December, his message is for every day of the year.

I know that many are frustrated by the whole thing of Santa, largely because of the overwhelming expectations and the overdoing of "stuff" for the kids. But that's not Santa's fault. It's what we created in our own minds.

Unfortunately, it's this overdone approach to Santa that we often share with our kids. I don't recall any book or movie in which Santa says, "The more stuff, and the more expensive, the better!" That was our creation, our misinterpretation of what it means to give.

The Santa I know is a lot more similar to Kris Kringle in *A Miracle on 34th Street*, the Santa who advocates sharing, connecting, laughing, blowing big bubbles with bubblegum, being a kid at heart, and above all continuing to believe. What does he want us to believe? He wants us to believe in the spirit of the season, in the joy of living from the center of our being instead of buying into the trappings of the world around us, and in the power of love and relationships.

Receiving toys and opening presents is great, but it's fleeting and only a small piece of the big picture. Santa reminds us to reconnect to our childlike awareness so that we notice the love and magic in our everyday lives.

At the end of the season, I put my decorations away and move toward the next big thing. But I keep a few Santa books out year-round. December may come and go, but Santa's message is always relevant.

What I remember feeling on Christmas Eve when I was eight or nine is one of those deeply ingrained experiences, a feeling of pure joy. I often find myself chasing those old feelings, though I'm beginning to recognize that certain types of joy are reserved for children. Nevertheless, whenever I see Santa or hear the bells, I'm reminded of the possibilities. I remember the true meaning of this time of year—or really, any time of year.

I'm comforted that my children can have a relationship with Santa way beyond their childhood. They can anticipate and have faith in the excitement and emotions that always reemerge at this time of year. They can appreciate that Santa reminds us to view the world in a more heart-centered and

NOTICE
Cathy Cassani Adams, LCSW, CPC, CYT

magical way.

Then, hopefully it will always be easy to believe.

SELF-LOVE

*You are the hero of your own story. The privilege of a lifetime
is being who you are.*

JOSEPH CAMPBELL

70

The difference between vanity and self-love

IN HER THIRD GRADE CLASS, my daughter is studying constellations. Last week she told me all about Cassiopeia, explaining that this particular constellation "bragged a lot." In fact, she was so excessively vain that it almost led to the death of her daughter, Andromeda, and eventually led to her own death. When she died, she was placed in the stars, where she is eternally forced to be upside down for half the year due to her vanity.

I remembered this story from my own school days. I remembered the mythology of Clash of the Titans. I also remembered the fear of being vain—the fear of letting anyone know you actually like yourself, a fear that kicks into high gear around middle school and unfortunately continues unless we become aware of it and let it go.

My immediate concern was that my daughter would mistake vanity for self-love. I didn't want her to think it was somehow a bad thing to fully love herself. Neither did I want her to imagine that loving herself could either harm others or cause her to have to hang upside down in oblivion.

"Do you know the difference between loving yourself and vanity?" I asked. Not too interested but willing to hear me out, she shrugged her shoulders.

"Self-love is when you understand you are good and just fine the way you are," I explained. "You don't need to shout it to other people, and you don't need other people's validation. You just know yourself to be exactly who you are supposed to be. You feel joy, share joy, and know deep down that this is exactly what you are supposed to do."

She was listening, so I continued, "Vanity is when you are unsure about your goodness, so you talk about it a lot and ask other people to confirm that you are indeed good. You constantly try to prove you are a good and loving person by aiming to be better than other people. It's because you don't fully trust who you are that you imagine the only way to experience joy is to be better than others. Do you see the huge difference between loving yourself and vanity?"

She smiled and, in her third grade way, said, "Yes, Mom." As I continued to look at her, I thought I saw a look of relief. Why relief? Probably because, deep down, she automatically feels self-love. We all do.

Life has a way of flowing when we love ourselves and trust who we are. Yes, there will be times when we question ourselves and perhaps even beat ourselves up. But we innately know that we are good, if for no other reason than that we are here. We don't need any validation beyond our own existence.

Self-love allows us to share love with the world. Lack of self-love, which as we've seen can show up as vanity, results in us asking the world to take care of us and blaming others for what we don't have. Lack of self-love is usually at the root of our relationship problems. Sometimes it disguises itself as other things, but lack of self-love is usually the source of our pain and the reason for our poor choices.

Believing in yourself is freedom. Not believing in yourself is the reason that you experience an emptiness in your life, even when you have what you thought you always wanted. What all of us seek is awareness of ourselves as loving beings.

In a nutshell, you are waiting for *you* to love you.

What greater gift can we give our children than to openly and unabashedly love ourselves? When they experience this in us, they are emboldened to hold onto their love of themselves, including the inner knowing and self-trust with which they were born.

Cassiopeia turns out to be a wonderful teacher. She wasn't inherently bad, she just wasn't aware she loved herself, and consequently asked the outside world to validate her. Despite her beauty and royalty, she didn't believe she was good enough.

If you look up in the night sky and see Cassiopeia upside down, send her some love and understanding. As you do so, allow your own self-love to flow in abundance.

SELF-LOVE

Cathy Cassani Adams, LCSW, CPC, CYT

71

Self-love is the key to all relationships

WHEN WE THINK OF LOVE, we tend to think romance, children, family, and friends. We love to love those we love. But what we may not realize is that our ability to be loving is sabotaged when we neglect self-love. If we haven't taken the time to love ourselves, our capacity for love is at a deficit.

When we harbor feelings of inadequacy, these become the lens through which we view the world, our experiences, and the people around us. For this reason, our ability to connect with another is limited by our ability to feel our own worth. Feeling negativity about who we are, and constantly criticizing our way of being, drains our energy and limits the love we have to offer.

To give love away, we must first feel it in our own skin. This is because we can't give away what we don't know we have. So if we want to be a good partner, we need to honor who we are. If we want our children to love themselves, we need to model what self-love looks like.

Not only society, but also the voice in your head will tell you that self-love is selfish or arrogant. But we need to question this outdated, backward way of thinking. The fact is, our choice to put ourselves last only decreases what we have to give. Indeed, it's this restricted sense of ourselves from a lack of self-love that's the true root of selfishness.

It's possible to create daily practices that reflect a dedication to self-love. For instance, spend time alone by saying no to things you don't want to do. Question the internal voice that criticizes. Spend time with people who make you smile. Enjoy inspirational music. Take a long bath. Laugh and play.

When the voice in your head insists you don't have time for self-love, recognize this as an old tape, a misinformed way of thinking that says you need to sacrifice yourself for others if you want to experience love. Such thinking is backwards, and it will keep you stuck in a cycle of searching without finding.

To love yourself is a moment-by-moment choice, an ongoing decision to recognize your worth and make yourself a priority. It's the ability to receive as equally as you give. It's also acceptance of your imperfections, inabilities, and confusion. Don't hold off on loving yourself until you have it all figured out and everything perfected. If you do, you'll spend a lifetime watching, waiting, and hoping.

Have you ever realized you are lovable with flaws? That you are worthy when you make mistakes? You are valuable simply because you're here.

Make self-love your top coping mechanism, your way of dealing with an often unpredictable and busy life. More importantly, recognize that it's the first and most essential step in connecting with those who most matter to you.

SELF-LOVE

Cathy Cassani Adams, LCSW, CPC, CYT

Are you fulfilling your obligation?

ONE OF MY DEAR FRIENDS made a comment that I can't get out of my head. "My dad taught me that we are obligated to live a good life, to give back in some way," she said.

This resonated so strongly with me, I literally *felt* the words when she said them.

I realize some of my readers may get hung up on the word "obligated." There's a feeling of defensiveness that arises whenever we're told we *have* to do something. But I view the word "obligated" as an invitation to *realize* ourselves—to figure out who we are so that we can share what we have.

Sharing what we have isn't always a business-creating or fame-seeking endeavor. Most of the time, sharing what we have simply means being real so that we can love others and practice joyful living.

Even joyful—*joy-filled*—living includes its share of challenges and mistakes. But these challenges and mistakes need to be seen as course correctors—signs that we need to go deeper inside to find a new direction. They are wake-up calls to get us off autopilot so that we can realign our lives.

We don't need to fear not being perfect. Rather, we can be

appreciative of ongoing reminders that perfection doesn't exist, and that striving to be externally validated doesn't hold a candle to feeling internally accepted and peaceful.

As we accept our humanness and experience peace, we get to share it. We get to smile at our kids when they run toward us, hold the door open for the person behind us, and hug someone who really needs a hug. We get to *be* what we are asking the world to be.

It's difficult to be kind to and accepting of others when we are at war within ourselves. When we are dealing with self-loathing or a lack of inner respect, this is what others will experience in our presence, since whatever we are full of is what tends to leak out of us.

This is when we need the most self-loving behavior of all, including a willingness to ask for help, the courage to state what we really need, and the openness to reach out to others for stabilization. The latter is such an important trait, because as much as we try, we can't do life alone. We are here to hold each other up. We are connected to help each other thrive.

The more we are truthful and ask for help, the more we feel the love of others. The more we feel the love of others, the more we want to give back. As we embrace our obligation to the world, we get to feel joy and also to share it.

As this way of being becomes a reality, everything changes. What we share has a ripple effect, and a loving ripple can create shifts beyond our comprehension. Non-loving ripples create shifts beyond our comprehension, too. We don't need any more evidence of their effects.

Internal awareness creates change, and this is how the planet becomes a better place for our kids. Not by pointing a finger at others or gossiping about the latest piece of news, but by shifting our focus inside and onto the present moment. We are powerful when we recognize who we are.

So instead of feeling obligated to do something for others, feel the obligation to yourself. Trust that you are worthy simply because you are here. Once you meet that self-obligation, you can't help but practice love because that's what lives underneath. It's your true being. The rest is just smoke, mirrors, disconnection, misunderstanding, and of course fear.

I wasn't surprised to hear these words about obligation from my friend this weekend. She's one of those true-blue people, an open book, a loving soul. She's always been self-accepting, and always placed tremendous value on truth and loyalty.

Her dad passed away when she was 18. I was with her at the time she found out. I love that she carries this wisdom from him inside her. It shows.

73

A letter to my daughter about self-love

LATELY YOU HAVE BEEN ASKING about your body, wondering about your size and shape, why you look the way you do, why others look different—important questions that I'm glad you asked. For now, this is my best answer:

You were born to be you. You aren't supposed to look like your sister, like me, or like any of your classmates. You might notice similarities, and that's fine. But you are unique. You are important to this world. You are supposed to be here. The design of your body is part of the greater plan of who you are. It should be no other way.

You may hear that you're supposed to look like this or that, or you may notice magazines or billboards that reflect a certain image. But they aren't real. They are people, just like you, who have been made up, dressed up, and airbrushed. None of this is reality—it's their work.

It's great to have a healthy body and feel good about how you look, but self-love isn't about falling in love with your appearance. It's about knowing your insides—your bliss, your gifts, your ability to share and experience joy.

Self-love will support you in every aspect of your life, since

SELF-LOVE
Cathy Cassani Adams, LCSW, CPC, CYT

people will treat you as you treat yourself. Because you love yourself, you won't allow others to take advantage of you. If someone decides to hurt you, you'll find support and begin the process of healing so that you can forgive—not to condone the behavior, but so that you don't carry around somebody else's pain.

Taking care of yourself is your most important job and the only way you'll have energy to take care of others. So don't waste time disliking yourself. Instead, spend time noticing your beauty. If you do, you'll see that everybody is beautiful. And you'll be surrounded by people and experiences that reflect this understanding.

I see you when you are happily lost in yourself—when you're laughing, singing, playing, and twirling. You shine so brightly that I get tears in my eyes. I feel your joy in being who you are, and I know this will always live inside you—even though at times you'll forget, because unfortunately we all do.

Your job is to have faith in the joy that's you, keeping in mind that it's not outside you. It's not in another person, not in your clothes, not in a job, and not in a grade or an award. It's only in you. And since only you can celebrate the ins and outs of being you, why not make it a celebration to remember?

At those moments when you forget, please come back and ask. I'm always here to remind you.

74

What I tend to forget over and over again

As I SIT BY THE OCEAN, humbled by the vastness, I think about the smallness of me. I think about when I used to play in the water as a kid, and how the tide would take me under. As scary and uncomfortable as those moments could be, I never questioned what was happening. I never fought against the idea that water was powerful and that I had little control.

Instead of fighting against what was, I would let go, which enabled me to find my way back to the surface so that I could breathe again. Naturally, I went right back to swimming and playing. Why? Because I accepted the ocean.

As an adult, I realize I exude little acceptance and have way too much knowledge, which causes me to focus on what could happen, why it could happen, why it shouldn't happen, and what I can do to keep it from happening. It's a case of less flow and more rules, and it leaves me feeling stiff and stunted.

I want more fluidity in my life—more ability to be taken down by a wave, then to swim to the surface with acceptance and a desire to learn from it and do it again.

The ocean reminds me of the limitations of my thinking. It reminds me how I can easily get stuck in a routine and value productivity over fun.

Though the water makes me feel small, paradoxically its bigness reminds me of my bigness. Everything in the ocean has a purpose, a role to play, and I know I too have an important role. My role is to be me, which is hard when I'm stiff, lost in thought, or caught up in an endless cycle of routine.

When I think about how uncountable others, so many of them no longer here, have peered at this ocean, I realize I have a limited time to play my role. I'm thankful to the water for reminding me I'm both small and big, and that certain things don't mean anything, while other things mean everything. Just like I'm thankful for the tree outside my window that reminds me not to be mad at the wind, but to stay grounded, accept it, and go with it. Or to each star that shines brightly without fear that its light will dim the light of other stars. There's an understanding that the collective shine is what makes the sky beautiful, and I'm in gratitude to everything that surrounds me for showing me what matters.

I'm also thankful to myself for walking away from a routine, even if it's for a day or two, to remember what I tend to forget.

75

When the teacher needs a teacher

ONE MORNING, I talked with my college students about how they need to take care of themselves so that they can best utilize their skills. Then in the middle of the day, I worked with elementary school students, going over with them how important it is for them to appreciate who they are and to make themselves a priority. Finally, in the evening, I worked with a group of preadolescent girls, discussing with them their value, and why their most important job is self-care.

In between these events, I dropped my kids off and picked them up, prepared meals, helped with homework, and cleaned up. By 9:30 p.m. I was seated in front of my computer, ready to read email and catch up on everything, when my nine-year-old daughter came up behind me. "Mom, I have something I have to show you," she announced.

"Can it wait until morning?"

"No."

I followed my daughter upstairs and she walked me into my bedroom. Pointing to my bed, she said, "Mom, this is your bed, and it needs you."

As I began to laugh and recite all the things I still needed

SELF-LOVE

Cathy Cassani Adams, LCSW, CPC, CYT

to do, she said, "Just wash your face, and I'll get you a water."

I listened. With lots of things still incomplete, I climbed into bed, only to be surprised by how quickly those things seemed minor—how, in reality, all of it could wait.

Then I hugged my daughter and said thank you, and she took her bear, turned off the light, and put herself to bed.

Sometimes the teacher needs a teacher.

Conclusion

YOUR CHILDREN DON'T WANT you to be perfect, they want you to be real. They desire a genuine connection combined with mutual respect for self and others. They want to be who they are and feel safe and affirmed in your presence. This sense of safety builds confidence, and this is what allows children to trust themselves and believe in what they can do.

Offering this sense of safety requires our self-awareness. Self-awareness isn't something we achieve once and for all, but is a daily practice of noticing ourselves. We practice being aware of our feelings and behavior, which in turn allows us to take responsibility for our lives. Instead of focusing on what others do or say, which is completely out of our control, we make choices for ourselves, deciding how to respond and participate. This is freedom, and this is what Gandhi was inferring when he told us to "*be* the change" we are looking for.

If we want our kids to know themselves and feel good about who they are, we have to demonstrate what this looks like. We have to stop believing that self-criticism and self-loathing are acceptable, and instead begin the practice of self-compassion and acceptance. Kids understand this at a very early age, as they share their feelings and trust their instincts. Sadly, we unconsciously steer them away from self-trust, focusing their attention on what society wants rather than allowing them to stay connected to their own internal guidance.

We use fear, guilt, shame, pain, and other outdated modes of behavior modification, thinking we are parenting, when in reality we are devaluing and controlling our children. As we do so, we unconsciously foster the development of a fierce inner critic in them—a pattern of negative self-talk that becomes a life-long saboteur. This is what leads to kids suppressing their feelings, living in fear, and numbing out with life-threatening substances and behaviors. When an individual's internal life is damaged, it dictates how we show up in the world. In other words, our behavior is a result of what we're feeling.

Self-awareness is essential, and it can be developed regardless of age. When I teach my social work and sociology students at Dominican University, self-awareness is the core of the curriculum. How is someone expected to help and understand others professionally unless they first understand themselves?

Self-awareness is the foundational principle of Zen Parenting Radio, a podcast that Todd and I host. Attachment theory has taught us that the best predictor of a child's well-being is a parent's self-understanding. For this reason, self-awareness is the underlying objective of every episode. Yet the message reaches beyond parents. We get emails from grandparents, young adults, and students who hear the underlying meaning and apply it to their current lives and experiences.

Be U, a conscious-living curriculum we created for kids, parents, and professionals revolves around self-awareness. How can a young girl or boy accept themselves if they don't know who they are? If they are always searching for what they don't have—things that so often are dictated to them by the media and society—they miss the experience and wonder of their own individuality. Rather than feeling the joy of flowing with their internal compass, they embark on a search for happiness through external means.

Self-awareness isn't just a parenting skill, but a life skill everyone benefits from. Due to the uniqueness of the parent-child relationship, parenting affords the ultimate opportunity to practice self-awareness. Our deep love for our children propels us to look into the mirror and take ownership of what we see.

This is a beautiful gift from our children. They are actually waking *us* up to our true nature, reminding us to go inside, see ourselves clearly, and heal what needs to be healed. They are extraordinarily talented in pointing out what we need to learn, even though this often involves discomfort, disagreements, and of course, extreme joy.

When we allow our children to be our teachers, they remind us of the value of seeing the world as they do, which involves living more simply, showing greater compassion, and being more mindful. We get to repay them by demonstrating how an adult can possess and practice these skills. And so the cycle continues.

CONCLUSION
Cathy Cassani Adams, LCSW, CPC, CYT

Cathy Adams, LCSW, CPC, CYT, serves as adjunct faculty in the sociology department at Dominican University, and she worked for many years as a Clinical Educator and Child and Family Therapist at Lurie Children's Hospital of Chicago. Known for her down-to-earth writing and presentation style, she co-hosts the internationally popular Zen Parenting Radio podcast (a finalist for Best Health and Lifestyle podcast in 2012 and 2013). She's a columnist for Chicago Parent Magazine (The Self-Aware Parent), and she's a regular parenting expert on WGN radio.

Her parent coaching has been the focus of a CBS News Report, as well as a Fox News Special Report, and she's been featured several times in *Parents Magazine, Newsweek Magazine, the Chicago Tribune, Ebony Magazine, Crain's Chicago Business, Today's Chicago Woman, and West Suburban Magazine.* She's a popular speaker at conferences and schools, and she runs self-awareness workshops for kids and adults.

As CEO of Be U, Inc., a conscious-living company, Cathy considers her most important experience to be that of mother to three girls.

CONNECT!

cathycassaniadams.com
facebook.com/selfawareparent
twitter.com/selfawareparent

and visit zenparentingradio.com.

LIVING WHAT YOU WANT YOUR KIDS TO LEARN
Cathy Cassani Adams, LCSW, CPC, CYT

CPSIA information can be obtained
at www.ICGtesting.com
Printed in the USA
FFOW01n2005250116
20623FF